Forever and Ever, Amen

The heart-warming stories
behind the music of Paul Overstreet

———◦◦◦———

PAUL OVERSTREET

Foreword by Randy Travis

Forever and Ever, Amen

*The heart-warming stories
behind the music of Paul Overstreet*

PAUL OVERSTREET

with
Jeanne Halsey

Treasure House

An Imprint of

Destiny Image® Publishers, Inc.
P.O. Box 310
Shippensburg, PA 17257-0310

"For where your treasure is, there will your heart be also."
Matthew 6:21

ISBN 0-7684-3007-0

For Worldwide Distribution
Printed in the U.S.A.

This book and all other Destiny Image, Revival Press,
MercyPlace, Fresh Bread, Destiny Image Fiction,
and Treasure House books are available at
Christian bookstores and distributors worldwide.

For a U.S. bookstore nearest you, call **1-800-722-6774**.
For more information on foreign distributors, call **717-532-3040**.
Or reach us on the Internet:
www.destinyimage.com

Paul Overstreet
Scarlet Moon Records
Post Office Box 320
Pegram, Tennessee 37143
www.pauloverstreet.com

———➤·◆·◄———

While we have diligently researched all the e-mails that were received on Paul's website, endeavoring to obtain accuracy and true representation, not all of the people were able to provide their complete information for verification. Therefore, most people are identified only by their first name and an initial for their surname, and some people also have their hometown mentioned. Since some of that information has not been available—yet their stories were simply too good to exclude—we have published them here anyway. Thank you in advance for your understanding…and enjoy the book!

—Jeanne Halsey

Dedication

I lovingly dedicate this book to the memory of my sister Brenda, whom we lost to cancer five years ago; to my wife, Julie; to our children—Nash, Summer, Chord, Harmony, Skye, and Charity—and to my mother, Mary Hatten; to my father, William "Bill" Overstreet, and to my brothers and sisters in Mississippi.

Acknowledgments

There are many people who inspired (and helped) me to write this book, and to them all, I give my sincerest thanks:

- Julie, without you there would be no book to write. Thank-you for your love, inspiration and all of the incredible effort you put into making this book happen

- The good people at *Destiny Image Publishers*—Don Nori, Don and Micki Milam—and Don Wise, for putting us together

- Jeanne, It is awsome how you took all my scattered thoughts and translated them into words that expressed what was burning in my heart and spirit. You are a life saver!!

- Our office personnel, for keeping me in touch with the right people

- Lisa Wysocky, for her energy and coordination

- My fellow songwriters: Jeff Borders, Tom Campbell, Claire Cloninger, Taylor Dunn, Jerry Michael, Don Moen, Thom Schuyler, Alan Shamblin, and Don Schlitz

- The fine Country artists who sang my songs: Glen Campbell, Paul Davis, the Forester Sisters, George Jones, Naomi and Wynonna Judd, Alison Krause, Susie Luchsinger, Jenny Morris, Michael Martin Murphy, Marie Osmond, Mel Tillis, Pam Tillis, Travis Tritt, Tanya Tucker, Randy Travis, the late Keith Whitley

- Don Finto, our first pastor, and the one who led us in our wedding vows

- Franklin Graham, for challenging me to stay straight with God

- Dennis Rainey, for challenging me to finish strong as a husband and father

- Beth Peters at *Copyright.net* , for helping with the videos for the DVD

- All those who have produced the records that have meant so much to others, James Stroud and Brown Banister

- *RCA Records,* for putting out all the songs that I recorded to radio, so people got a chance to hear them

- All those who have prayed for my family and myself over the years.

- My mom, Mary Hatten, who believed me when (at age 4) I said I knew I was going to be a singer of some kind…for selling her piano to buy the Ovation guitar that I brought to Nashville…and for taking me to Little Rock, Arkansas, to record my first demo when I was a senior in high school

- My brother Wiley Overstreet, for letting me move in with him for a couple of years so I could play football…and for giving me the car that I drove to Nashville

- My brother Norman Overstreet, for teaching me some guitar chords in California…and always embarrassing me by making me sing at the strangest places

- My sister Edith Goff, for always telling me that I could do anything

- My brother-in-law Ronnie Goff, for showing me more guitar chords

- My dad, William "Bill" Overstreet, for having me sing, at age 8 or 9, at an ice cream gathering at my Uncle Curtis's house, and for the first time getting money for doing it (after they passed the hat)

- My Aunt Berna, who died February 19,1999—one of the great encouragers in my life

- So many others who have encouraged me along the way

- And to all the wonderful, generous people who logged on to *www.pauloverstreet.com* to share their stories for this book!

Endorsements

"Over the past couple of years, Paul Overstreet has become a good friend. He is a man of kindred spirit in calling our nation's families back to Jesus Christ. His songs not only bring a smile to my face and refresh my soul, but they define *real* family values. *Forever and Ever, Amen* will tickle your funny bone, touch your heart and realign your family values! If you like Paul's songs, you'll love this book!"

—**Dennis Rainey**
Executive Director, *Family Life*

"Paul Overstreet, like many of us, is an example of God's grace. I have had the privilege of working with him around the world and have been impressed with his enormous talent and sincerity. Paul Overstreet has penned some of the greatest songs in country music history. But what is most exciting to me is the fact that he has used his gift to also write songs that point people to the Lord Jesus Christ. One of my all-time favorites is 'God Is Good.'

I thank the Lord for the 'song of praise' that He put in the heart of Paul Overstreet. Thanks, Paul, for allowing God to speak through your music to encourage home and family—and most of all to publicly testify of God's everlasting love."

—**Franklin Graham**
Chief Executive Office, Billy Graham Evangelistic Association
President, Samaritan's Purse

"In a world where men have forgotten how to be real, Paul's songs are trail markers toward resurrecting a man's heart. Whether in 'Seein'

My Father in Me' among men, 'We've Got to Keep on Meeting Like This' among couples, or 'One In a Million' among singles, he teaches us to honor our longings and celebrate our joys."

—**Gordon Dalbey**
Conference speaker and author of *Healing the Masculine Soul*

"The Bible says 'Out of the overflow of the heart the mouth speaks' (Mt. 12:34). This rings true of Paul's songwriting, as his music is an accurate reflection of his character. Something of Paul's gentle and humble nature, his faith in God, and his love for his precious wife, Julie, radiates through every song performed.

The music and harmony of Paul Overstreet's words and life bless my household and heart. In an industry and world of compromises, Paul has stayed true to his faith, his love, and his zeal for life."

—**Steve Wisniewski**
#76 Oakland Raiders

"In late 1997 I had the privilege of meeting Paul Overstreet at the close of one of our Sunday morning services at The Oasis Church here in Nashville, Tennessee. Of course, I had been a fan of Paul's great songwriting for several years, and was delighted that he was visiting our young church. We talked briefly and I thought that might be the last time I would see him. To my delight he was back in a few weeks with his precious wife, Julie, and their beautiful family. Over the last few years they have become a vital part of the Oasis congregation, and in the process our families have become very close.

Paul Overstreet is a man of great integrity. For several years I've watched him navigate the emotional and often turbulent waters of the country music industry. Never once have I known of his compromising his faith. He models the living Christ in everything he does—his songs, his daily life, and most of all, his family, He is a real man of God and my admiration for him runs deep.

Paul Overstreet is, in my opinion, one of the greatest songwriters of our time. He captures feelings, images, and truth and weaves them together in a style that is distinctly his own. There is a great passage in the Bible that comes to mind when I think of Paul. 'A good man out of the good treasure of his heart brings forth good things' (Mt. 12:35 NKJ). Paul is surrounded by the goodness of God and it is a glorious reflection of the good heart that beats inside this poet minstrel. I am honored that Paul would call me his pastor, and I'm honored to call Paul my friend."

—**Danny Chambers**
Senior Pastor, The Oasis Church
Nashville, Tennessee

"It is with great pleasure that I introduce you to my friend, Paul Overstreet. Paul is a rare talent—part poet, part country boy. He takes what we often feel in our hearts and puts it in words and song. No doubt you already know many of his compositions, even if you've never heard Paul himself sing. That's because many of Country music's top artists have recorded a song or two from Paul Overstreet. I'm sure this book will challenge, encourage, comfort, and touch your heart, as Paul has touched mine and many others."

—**Greg Laurie**
Senior Pastor, Harvest Christian Fellowship

"Having known Paul for several years and been so impressed and inspired by his music and creative abilities, I'm thrilled with the wonderful ministry potential of this book. I am privileged to recommend it."

—**Norm Miller**
Chairman, Interstate Batteries

"When I heard my first Paul Overstreet song and instinctively started singing along, I knew I had found a 'friend of the family' in Nashville. It was refreshing to hear the words and music of home and family from a headliner artist and award winning songwriter. When I learned Paul is a fellow home school dad, I was a fan for life. Now that my children are taking up the acoustic cause, the only question left is who will get my complete Paul Overstreet CD collections! Keep writing, Paul."

—**Clay Clarkson**
Executive Director, Whole Heart Ministries
Author, *Educating the Wholehearted Child*
Columnist, national speaker on home school education

Table of Contents

Foreword xv

Introduction xvii

Chapter 1   "Forever and Ever, Amen" 1

Chapter 2   "Seein' My Father in Me" 11

Chapter 3   "I Won't Take Less Than Your Love" 23

Chapter 4   "A Long Line of Love" 29

Chapter 5   "Love Helps Those Who Cannot Help Themselves" . . .37

Chapter 6   "All the Fun" .43

Chapter 7   "Sowin' Love" .49

Chapter 8   "Dig Another Well" 57

Chapter 9   "Richest Man on Earth" 65

Chapter 10 "(She Wants to Be a) Homemaker" 73

Chapter 11 "Heroes" 83

Chapter 12 "Daddy's Come Around (to Mama's Way of Thinking)" . .93

Chapter 13 "When You Say Nothing at All" 101

Chapter 14 "Ball and Chain" 109

Chapter 15 "Billy Can't Read" 115

Chapter 16 "What's Going Without Saying" 121

Chapter 17 "'Til the Mountains Disappear" 129

Chapter 18 "One in a Million" 137

Chapter 19 "The Day My Daddy Didn't Come Home" 143

Chapter 20 "God Is Good (All the Time)" 151

Table of Contents

(continued)

More "Fan Mail" 159
More "Photos" 175
Epilogue 179
Paul's Songs 185
Resources: Discography & Videology 191
Paul's Picks 193
Video CD Instructions 199

Foreword

Let me begin with an example of the gift Paul has as a writer. It was the first time we were to work together on a song. We sat down, he took his guitar in hand and said, "I had an idea on the way over," and then began to sing—not just a couple of lines—but the first verse and a complete chorus! I felt like someone hired to take notes but couldn't keep up! Luckily, there was a tape player in "Record" mode. Needless to say, I was impressed.

If I had to pick my favorite Overstreet song, it would have to be "Forever and Ever, Amen." The response we've received in person and by mail from this one song outweighs all others I've recorded, combined. This song has made people laugh, cry, remember loved ones who are no longer with them, and consider how much they love those who are still around. I have no idea how many times people have told me this song was used at their wedding, or how many times it's been used at funerals.

One story I'll tell which was very special. A man wrote a letter about his wife who was going through chemotherapy, had lost her hair, and was not dealing with this very well. He told how they got in the car, he turned on the key, and had the tape cued to the lyrics:

"They say time takes its toll on a body,
Makes a young girl's brown hair turn gray;
Well, honey, I don't care, I ain't in love with your hair,
And if it all fell out, I'd love you anyway."

Then the letter goes on to tell how she started crying, and how after that, she seemed to deal with what she went through with a far better outlook. As the singer of this song, this story made me feel I'd done something right. As the writer of the song, Paul must feel the same…and far more.

Over the years, I've recorded quite a few Paul Overstreet songs. It seems like Paul has this wonderful ability to step back and observe family, relationships, and life in general (good times and bad), and write down what he sees and feels. The outcome has been an amazing body of work, with songs that have touched people of all ages and all walks of life. I consider myself very fortunate each time I stand before an audience and sing his songs. More often than any other time, I see the powerful effect his words have on people.

Randy Travis

Introduction

I am a regular guy. I get up in the morning, I brush my teeth, I kiss my wife, I play with my kids…and I write songs. I don't actually set out to write songs that are going to profoundly change people's lives—but sometimes, somehow, that just seems to work its way into the mix. For some reason, God has seen it is important to get involved in my song-writing…but most of the time, I didn't even know it. It would be much later—when I heard stories from people around the country—that I would realize that God had used a song in a special way.

While reading the stories sent to my website (and contained in this book), it dawned on me, "There is a lot more going on here than I know!" I love it when God does something like that. He takes a couple of old regular people, puts a gentle hand on them, and does something that impacts other lives. I guess He did something like that with some plain old fishermen long ago.

That's where the inspiration for this book came. I wanted to share some of the hundreds of true stories submitted by my friends from around the world, to let them tell how some of those songs affected their lives. I don't really believe it was because of my co-writers or me—a lot of times, we didn't have a clue what was going to happen with a song…we were just doing our jobs! Sometimes, just showing up for work is the most important thing we can do in a day.

I now believe that music and songs have an unusual power to reach into the hearts and souls of human beings, so we continue to write songs. We do our best to be thoughtful of that power, and try to do something good with the gifts we've been given…and the time that others give us by listening to our songs. Maybe that's why God sometimes gets involved, making the songs much more important than they would be ordinarily.

I used to write songs that were about the misery in my own life. Even if there wasn't a lot, I'd make some up. It just seemed to be what Country music was about. But then I read in the Bible where it says, "As [a man] thinks in his heart, so is he" (Prov. 23:7a)—and I felt that God was directing me to the kind of songs He wanted me to write. It was at that point that I made a decision to start saying good things about my own life. It's a really thin line you walk—writing songs that are positive, yet keeping them from sounding "hokey" or trite—while saying something important.

I remember saying to God once—when referring to "I Fell in Love Again Last Night" and others like it—"Well, God, I think these songs are too good for Country music," because they were talking about positive things, and I knew the attitude on Music Row toward that kind of writing. I immediately felt as though He was speaking to my heart, saying, "Trust Me"…so I did.

I was raised with a Christian background. That means—like anybody else—my life went through a lot of twists and turns. When I was 29 years old, I had to take a serious look at my life and make a decision, "Am I going to continue on the road of what I want to do…or am I going to finally try to learn what God wants me to do?" I decided that I had done everything I had wanted to do for so long, and I wasn't happy and it was getting worse. So I was ready for God to take over.

I first thought He was going to have me become a missionary in Africa, or preach in a small country church, or something like that. Surely He would want me to only sing and write Christian music! I was totally shocked when He started directing me to write Country songs with a different message than I had been writing. He closed all the doors to the Christian music direction at that time. Wow, was I confused! But I just wanted to follow Him. I guess that's what people mean when they talk about putting God in a box—I realized I didn't know God very well.

That doesn't mean that the rest of my life is going to be nothing but smooth sailing. But it does mean that He is always going to be the Captain of my ship. No matter what else happens in my life—whether I love my wife, or argue with her...or our kids are great, or causing a lot of trouble...or our bank account is full, or flat...or I have a great career, or one that crashes—Jesus Christ makes my life worthwhile. I receive my self-worth from Him. I also get to share my success with Him. He is the reason for it, and the reason I can do what I do.

And I really thank God that He didn't let me go totally into Gospel music at that time! Instead, He placed me and my songs into secular Country music, where the message of the songs could speak to a whole different audience, where people who wouldn't otherwise plan to listen to Christian music could still hear God speaking to them. They might be drawn closer to Him, and might be able to hear Him saying something special, just for them, because of these songs. It has been a tremendously rewarding experience for me.

Paul Overstreet

Kingston Springs, Tennessee

January 2001

Kids sitting on "the" porch—Summer, Chord, Skye (holding six-week-old Charity), Harmony, and Nash. Father's Day, 1999

Chapter 1

Forever and Ever, Amen

When Julie and I were just married, my mom came to visit. Julie was working at a hair salon then, and she took my mom with her to work. Before they left, I said, "Whatever you do, Julie, don't mess up Mom's hair. I know you're going to take her down there and experiment on her." Mom told Julie that she had a bad permanent where they "fried" her hair, and Julie was going to help correct it. I warned, "Don't cut her hair too short, don't color it green or something." Well, I'll be darned if Mom didn't come home with her hair cut shorter than mine and tinted a sort of green color! I thought, "This is not a good step in the right direction for a new wife and a mother-in-law!"

At that time, there was an annual golf tournament for the music industry in Nashville called The Acuff-Rose Tournament.

Verse One

You may think that I'm talking foolish,

You've heard that I'm wild and I'm free;

You may wonder how I can promise you now

This love that I feel for you always will be.

You're not just time that I'm killing,

I'm no longer one of those guys.

As sure as I live, this love that I give

Is going to be yours until the day I die.

Chorus One

I'm going to love you
forever,

Forever and ever, amen.

As long as old men sit and
talk about the weather,

As long as old women sit
and talk about old men.

If you wonder how long
I'll be faithful,

I'll be happy to tell
you again;

I'm going to love you
forever and ever,

Forever and ever, amen.

Verse Two

They say time takes its
toll on a body,

When a young girl's brown
hair turns gray;

Well, honey, I don't care, I
ain't in love with your hair;

And if it all fell out,
I'd love you anyway.

Well, they say time can
play tricks on a memory;

Make people forget
things they knew.

I was playing in the tournament with a group of songwriters and friends. We played all day, and I was tired. As I finished, I called home to check in, and Julie said that Don Schlitz was looking for me, saying he had something about a song idea. So I called Don; he was really excited about this idea and wanted to write that night. I tried to put it off, but then thought better about it.

I got home, got a bite to eat and then Don showed up. He told me about his little boy who had been learning to say the "Lord's Prayer." He had been going around the house saying, "Forever and ever, amen," at the end of everything. He'd say, "Mommy, I love you, forever and ever, amen." Don thought it made a great idea for a song.

So we began working on the song. It was flowing really smoothly. When we got to the third verse, I told Don about the story of Mom and Julie…and when the song starts to say: *Time takes a toll on a body, makes a young girl's brown hair turn gray*— we originally toyed with the color green, in honor of Julie and Mom! We laughed a little, decided on gray, and then moved on.

Randy Travis had a big hit with this song, taking it to the top of the charts and selling a ton of records. It was nominated for a Grammy Award. In 1987, we traveled to New York, checked in at a fancy hotel, and were having fun in the big city. At the Awards show, there were all kinds of music celebrities—Stevie Wonder, Michael Jackson (just coming out with that "moon-walking" dance number he was to perform on the show that night)—a star-studded line-up. I got up to go to the bathroom during the show…and the usher wouldn't let me go back to my seat because they were "on the air." That's when the Michael Jackson dance segment was going on, so I missed it!

Our category came up, and I got nervous as could be. Just before we went to the Awards show, I had taken time to pray—I knew it was going to be an important night and I didn't want to look like a complete idiot—so I asked God for a little humor or something to help if we were to be the winners. Well, we *did* win. Don went first, and he did a great job speaking…then it was my turn. The first thing out of my mouth was, "I'd like to thank my wife and kids, they're back at the motel." Everybody in Radio City Music Hall started laughing, but I didn't know why. I thought they were laughing because I *was* sitting with a woman, and I thought they were thinking, "What kind of guy would bring his wife all the way to New York, and then leave her in the room!" So I tried to straighten it out, saying, "No, my wife is here. The kids are back at the motel." They laughed even harder.

When I got back to our room, my wife's cousin, who lived in New York then, was waiting, and he knew why they were laughing. He said, "Paul, there *are* no 'motels' in Manhattan!" I was humiliated. All night

Well, it's easy to see,
it's happening to me;

I've already forgotten
every woman but you.

Chorus Two

I'm going to love you
forever,

Forever and ever, amen.

As long as old men sit and
talk about the weather,

As long as old women sit
and talk about old men.

If you wonder how long
I'll be faithful,

Just listen to how
this song ends;

I'm going to love you
forever and ever,

Forever and ever, amen.

Tag

Yes, I'm going to love
you forever and ever,

Forever and ever,
forever and ever,

Forever and ever, amen.

long, I tried to talk myself out of being depressed. I thought I had done a good job...until I got to the front desk the next morning. The little girl behind the desk said, "I saw you on TV last night." I thought, "With all those stars on there, why would she remember me?" Then she said, "Yeah, you called the New York Hilton a motel!" I wanted to hide. Then she added, "You were joking, right?" I wanted to lie and agree with her...but at that moment, I remembered my prayer of the night before and realized that God had given me what I had prayed for—although I never thought He would use my ignorance. You have to be careful what you pray for!

Randy Travis once sent over a letter from a family who had a little girl who had been going through chemotherapy, and

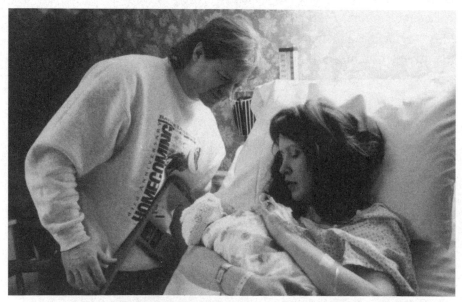

A proud Papa—Paul and Julie with Skye

she had lost all her hair. She wasn't going out to play with her friends because she was ashamed and embarrassed. But when she heard Randy Travis, this big star, singing, *"If all your hair fell out, I'd love you anyway"*...then she decided at that moment that if Randy Travis could love somebody without any hair, then her friends could love her without any hair too. That helped her make the decision to go out and play, and try to resume her normal life.

There is one other thing about this song: it has a universal message. I was in Australia with Franklin Graham, and I sang this song to a group of people at a governmental meeting. They weren't familiar with my music—or American Country music, for that matter—yet they were following the song, they were interested, it made perfect sense to them. Whether a song is a hit or not, if it has impact—when it gets people right in the heart—then I know it's a good song.

Letters

⟫━◦━⟪

≈ She Knew What Was Missing ≈

When I was a child, I had accepted the Lord Jesus as my Savior, and stayed with the Lord until I joined the Navy when I was 21. The lifestyle of the Navy appealed to me, and I "strayed from the flock," to put it nicely. I stayed

About Paul Overstreet

Paul's Boyhood in Mississippi

Paul Overstreet was born in Newton, Mississippi, but grew up in the small town of Vancleave, Mississippi, the youngest of five children born to William and Mary Overstreet. His dad, William (or "Bill," as most knew him), preached in small Baptist churches around southern Mississippi and Louisiana. Everyone in Paul's family had musical talent: his oldest brother sang like a 1950s rock star; his sisters played the piano and sang '60's music; his next-to-the-oldest brother played the guitar and sang; his mom played the piano and sang; Dad sang too, and led the singing at church.

(More about Paul Overstreet in Chapter 2)

"When my mother was dying from cancer, she was taking chemo treatments and had little to no hair. My three children would sing to her the song, 'Forever and Ever, Amen.' She would always smile, it always lifted

in the Navy for about eight years, and during this time I knew loneliness, heartbreak, and knew that something was missing. I had grown up with a Christian family, knew what it was like to have loving parents, and I wanted that kind of life for myself and my future husband. So I did all I could do to find that man, to no avail.

Then I heard "Forever and Ever, Amen." I knew that was what was missing from every relationship that I had had, God and the "forever and ever" part. I put my body and mind to the task but did not put my soul and my Lord to it. That was about the time that I got into a little trouble, and I put my life back into Jesus' hands. I broke down and prayed to the Lord, and confessed all that I had done—not that He didn't know already, but I needed to tell Him. I then told God that I would look no more and would put my fate in His hands.

I was able to do that, and within one month, I met my future husband. I knew on our first date that this was the man whom God had given me, and we were married a year and a half later. He has been a blessing to my life. Thanks to the "Forever and Ever" song that brought me back to my senses, and my upbringing with Jesus, I have that "forever and ever, amen"! Thank you, Paul, for writing that song which turned me back around to be back with Jesus. We attended the "I Still Do" conference in Houston, and it was fantastic, a great renewal to me and my marriage.

—**Laura D.; Corpus Christi, Texas**

≈ No Matter What ≈

*W*hen my mother was dying from cancer, she was taking chemo treatments and had little to no hair. My three children would sing to her the song, "Forever and Ever, Amen." She would always smile, it always lifted her spirits, she always knew we all loved her, no matter what, and that God was with her all the way home. This song means so much to my children and me. Thank you and God bless you.

—Linda G.; Aurora, Indiana

≈ Monumental Impact ≈

*A*pril 16, 1989, Sonya and I started dating. Sonya didn't care for Country music much. I sang "Forever and Ever, Amen" to her one day, and she's been hooked on Country music ever since (now she is my wife). Her Country CD collection is bigger than my cassette and album collection has ever been. "Forever and Ever, Amen" has been our song for 11 years now. On May 20, 2000, Sonya and I attended [Family Life's] "I Still Do" conference at the Anaheim Pond in California, where you sang "our song" and then signed as witness to our reaffirmation of the wedding covenant. Also, "Seein' My Father in Me" has a monumental impact on my life as a son and a father also. Thank you, Paul, for following Jesus, and helping Him to lead others to our Father God! His presence and power is evident in your life, and you are an inspiration to us, as you have been to me since the late 1970s. May God bless you

> *her spirits, she always knew we all loved her, no matter what, and that God was with her all the way home."*

Awards

BMI
Songwriter of the Year
for 1987, 1988, 1989,
1990, and 1991

"Now that I understand how God will love me forever because of my faith in Jesus Christ, I can now believe my husband can too. Thank you for writing that song, and for singing it at the conference. I have confidence

and yours with continued success. I do thank God for His gift of you to the world.

—Leon T.; Costa Mesa, California

∾ An Ordinary Man Using God-Given Talent ∾

*I*n 1987, my boyfriend (now my husband) and I were sitting on my couch at my mother's house watching the Country Music Awards. You were up to win an award for the song, "Forever and Ever, Amen." Michael said, "This is the man we want to win [the award]; he's a Christian." I replied, "Yeah, they all try to make you think that by putting God into their acceptance speech." He answered, "Paul is different. Yes, he will thank God, but you will also know that he is very sincere." As we all know, you won. Yes, you made your little joke at the beginning and you did thank God, but you didn't stop there. You shared a brief testimony of how God changed your life. I was shocked. You don't see that very often. Both of us in tears, we cheered you on. I remember this time so well because after your speech, Michael said that "Forever and Ever, Amen" would be our song. He then asked me to go steady. He vowed that night that if we were ever aware of you performing close by, that he would take me to see you.

In our 12 years of marriage that had not happened until the "I Still Do" conference in Memphis, Tennessee. The emotions that were felt by both of us were overwhelming. It was like we were 17 and 20 again. Our song is still "Forever and Ever, Amen." You are a hero to us in the way that you share your relationship with God publicly and in your songs. God has used many of your songs to influence our lives. For me, the song, "Homemaker," is priceless. God uses it in a way to remind me of my role as a wife and mother when I am down or discouraged. It's a good feeling to have, while driving down the road, knowing that our three children are hearing and singing these songs and are being taught at a very young age what their role some day will be in relationships. Paul Overstreet is an ordinary man using the God-given talents to make a difference in our world. I can only hope that others will see what God has done in your life, and desire the same for theirs.

—**Lisa T.; Paragould, Arkansas**

"Forever Love"

I had never heard of Paul Overstreet until I went to the "I Still Do" conference from Family Life Ministries in Houston, Texas, although a few years ago I had heard of his song, "Forever and Ever, Amen." Before my husband and I were married, this was a special song my husband told me about. Later, I became a Christian and did not keep up with secular music. At the conference, Paul played that song, and it meant so much to me. It was like God gave me a special present that day through Paul singing that song, because I had

in the 'forever-ness' of God's love, and He shows it in my husband's unconditional 'forever' love that he has for me."

*"**Forever and Ever, Amen**" was included on the album,* **A Songwriter's Project— Volume One**, *released in August 2000, along with these additional songs:*

Same Ole Me

I Won't Take Less Than Your Love

When You Say Nothing at All

A Long Line of Love

Diggin' Up Bones

Be Mine

On the Other Hand

I Fell in Love Again Last Night

Toughest Battles

What Are Friends For

When Mama Ain't Happy

(BMG Music; RCA Corporation)

---

not heard it since before we were married—yet it always had a special place in my heart. Before Gregg and I were married, when he would tell me he would love me forever, that "forever" business just seemed so hard for me to believe. Now that I understand how God will love me forever because of my faith in Jesus Christ, I can now believe my husband can too. Thank you for writing that song, and for singing it at the conference. I have confidence in the "forever-ness" of God's love, and He shows it in my husband's unconditional "forever" love that he has for me. Keep up the good work, and remember that because you are His, you are the salt and the light in the world (Mt. 5:13-14).

—**Lisa Van K.; Humble, Texas**

❧ Engraved Into His Ring ❧

*One song that my husband and I have always considered "our song" is "Forever and Ever, Amen," as recorded by Randy Travis. It became a favorite while we were dating, and we used it in our wedding. I even had "Forever, Amen" engraved inside my husband's wedding band! That said, I was **so** happily surprised to find out several years later that it was written by Paul Overstreet! Thank you, Paul!*

—**Lorraine P.**

Chapter 2

Seein' My Father in Me

Taylor Dunn had been working with the construction company that was remodeling our attic, turning it into a bedroom, when the man who ran the company suggested I listen to some of Taylor's songs. I did listen, and believed he had a lot of potential, so we signed him to our publishing company. (You always hear about these kinds of stories happening in Nashville, and this is another one!)

I was starting on my first solo album for *MTM Records,* and just before we went into the studio the first day, Taylor shared this idea he had for a song, *"Seein' My Father in Me."* Taylor had a good relationship with his dad, although they had gone through some tough times—but I had not had the same kind of consistent relationship with my dad. However, as he told me about his idea, I suddenly got a vision of

Verse One

Last night, we brought
the children by

To visit their Grandpa,

And it's plain to see
they're truly part of him.

While waiting there,
their Grandma

Pulled out some old
photographs,

And he sure looked a lot
like me back then.

Chorus One

I'm seeing my father
in me,

I guess that's how it's
meant to be;

And I find I'm more and
more like him each day.

I notice I walk
the way he walks,

I notice I talk
the way he talks;

I'm starting to see
my father in me.

Verse Two

And today I took my
wife for a walk

Down that old dirt road

Where my Daddy took
my Mom so many times.

And we found the time
to mention things

We never had before,

And we shared
some thoughts

About the family life.

how the song could be written. At that moment, I didn't know that it would be part of a real healing process for me.

When I was a kid, I used to look at pictures of my dad and try to see things about me that were similar to him—and I liked seeing parts of myself that looked like him. My mom and dad had divorced when I was about six years old; he moved to California, and I stayed with my mom in Mississippi. As I got older and he wasn't around, I started hearing people talk about him. All I knew about him was from the stories I heard and the little time I spent with him a few summers. Something started changing in me, and I began to become a person who didn't want to be like him. When he was around, I felt like he shouldn't have any say in my life at all, since he hadn't been there for me when I needed him. There was a root of bitterness growing inside of me, but I didn't know it.

When I was grown up, I thought I had already dealt with all these issues about my childhood and my father, that I was tough inside and really didn't have any hard feelings toward my dad...or any feelings, one way or the other. No matter what, I was not going to be able to recapture those years that had gone by.

A lot of things could have made life easier for me if my dad had been around. During some of those summers I spent with him in California, I recognized that it was an important thing for a boy to have a dad. I didn't care if he was rich or poor, it just was good to hang around him, throw a baseball, go fishing, build an old car together...just anything! I guess that's why I want to be there for my sons so much, because I know what it's like when a kid doesn't have a dad around.

As I became a man, I started seeing things that I needed to know but hadn't learned while growing up. When I started reading the Bible, I found a verse that made all the difference in the world to me, where God said He is "a Father [to] the fatherless" (Ps. 68:5). I dug into that with all the faith I could find! "Could this really be true? God will be my Father?" If so, I had just found the greatest Father there could ever be! The truth is: God will be a Father to us all if we'll let Him.

Bridge

Now looking back,
I can recall

The times when
we disagreed,

When I could not take hold
of his old-fashioned ways;

And the more I tried to
prove him wrong,

The more I proved
him right;

Now I know why he
still stood by me

When I went through
that stage.

"Seein' My Father in Me" by Paul Overstreet and Taylor Dunn. Scarlet Moon Music (BMI). 1988.

Paul with his dad, Summer (23 months), Nash (3), and Chord (4 months). Paul's dad came to Nashville for the filming for the "Seein' My Father in Me" video.

About Paul Overstreet

Hard Times Growing Up

After his parents divorced, there were hard times. "I was about six years old at the time. There were weeks we didn't know where our food would come from," Paul remembered. "Mom cried a lot, prayed a lot, trying to figure out a way to take care of her family. I also remember standing in line with Mom to get commodities—government-dispersed food supplies like cheese, peanut butter, lard, flour. Mom remarried, and things changed a bit."

(More about Paul Overstreet in Chapter 3)

One of the things God did for me when I accepted Him was to restore my relationship with my earthly father. I know we don't have the same relationship we could have had if we had been around each other all those years, but it's still very good. He's a great guy, and I love him. We have come a long way, have spent some good times together…and I've come to a place where I don't judge him, I just love him. I may not agree with all the roads he has chosen, but that's between him and God.

When I went into the studio for that first album, all I had was a verse and a chorus for this song. I played them for the producer, James Stroud, and he loved it. He wanted to record it the next day, so Taylor and I had to finish it up in order to record it! When this song was chosen to the single and a video, Julie had the idea to use a lot of different fathers and sons, which was a great idea. If you watch the video, you'll see that some of the fathers and sons were a little uncomfortable with each other…because some had not been speaking to each other, or their relationships were strained for some reason or another. I also asked my dad to be with me and my children, and he did.

This song turned out to be my first number-one record. But more than that, it holds a philosophy that really expresses my desire for my family. One day, I want my children to be able to say, *"I'm happy to see my father in me."*

Letters

❧ Saying What Most People Can't ❧

My dad was, is, and always will be my hero. From the first time I heard this song, it put a lump in my throat because I felt this was our story. Every word fits him and me from when I was little, those terrible teens, and even as an adult. He's the greatest man who ever walked the earth. We lost him in January 2000 to cancer at age 60. With all the things happening, the first song that came to mind to play at his funeral was this one. It was the only way we could tell him how much we loved him. There wasn't a dry eye because the song means something to everyone. At first, it was sad to listen to it, but I find comfort in your song. My family and I will always cherish and treasure this song in our hearts. Thank you for saying what most people can't.

—**Kristy W.**

❧ Earthly Father and Heavenly Father ❧

When I was a teenager, the song, "Seein' My Father in Me," really got me thinking about my father and our relationship. I was just entering the rebellious stage of my life. The verse in the song—"The more I tried to prove him wrong, the more I proved him right"—really said something to me.

But I moved out of my father and stepmother's house into my mother's house a state away.

"My family and I will always cherish and treasure this song in our hearts. Thank you for saying what most people can't."

"Seein' My Father in Me"
was included on the album,
Sowin' Love,
released in 1989, along
with these additional songs:

Love Helps Those
Who Cannot Help
Themselves

All the Fun

Call the Preacher

Richest Man on Earth

Sowin' Love

Love Never Sleeps

Dig Another Well

What God Has Joined
Together

Homemaker

'Neath the Light
of Your Love

(BMG Music; RCA Corporation)

My father and stepmother (who was more of a mom than my birth mother) were (and still are) very good Christians, and at the time, I thought they were being very strict with me because I was the oldest child. However, my mother would let me do what I wanted to do. I was able to go to parties and have more freedom, I thought.

That first summer, I met my future wife—we knew right away that we were supposed to be together. We got married young (she was 19, I was 18), and we thought we had life all figured out. But by January 1996, I thought we were going to divorce. However, **God** had other plans, because that month, my wife told me she was pregnant. That was when my father's teachings and ethics really started to show, and I started to see my father in me. I couldn't leave my wife alone with a child to raise, so we stayed together for the child's sake.

In May 1996, my wife and I both accepted the Lord Jesus Christ into our lives and our marriage. Then my father and I really got to know each other. Not only did I see my earthly father in me, but I began to see my Heavenly Father in me too. My father wasn't trying to be strict with me, he was trying to protect me from the same mistakes he had made.

My wife and I have been saved for over four years, and we have a little girl who is truly a gift from God. As the years went on after I got saved, your songs kept popping up and began to have more meaning for me.

—**James M.; Albion, Indiana**

Made a Difference ❦

*M*y father was diagnosed with lung cancer, although he had not smoked for over 40 years. It was a difficult time for his family. None of us had any idea what would happen to Dad; no one in our family had ever been afflicted with cancer. In searching for any way I could calm our family members—especially my mom and Dad himself—I put together an audio tape with many of the Country songs I loved that related to fathers, family and faith. At the top of the list was a song that always moves me, "Seein' My Father in Me." Dad has always been my idol. I know I can never measure up to him, but a lot of the same characteristics he possesses, I see in myself—maybe there is still hope for me! "Heroes" and "The Richest Man on Earth" were also included on that tape—all very descriptive of Dad and our relationship. Over the past year, he has listened often to the tape, especially every time he goes to the hospital for treatment. After nearly a year of chemotherapy and radiation therapy, we are happy to announce that Dad is stronger and will make it to his 80th birthday. He often speaks of the tape, especially the Paul Overstreet songs, as being very calming and therapeutic. We want to thank Paul for his very sensitive renditions, describing very real relationships between loving family members. It has made a great difference in my life, and may very well have extended the life of my father. Thank you.

—**Eron G.; Oakdale, California**

"Not only did I see my earthly father in me, but I began to see my Heavenly Father in me too. My father wasn't trying to be strict with me, he was trying to protect me from the same mistakes he had made."

—————⊷❖⊶—————

"*Hearing this soon after the birth of my first son filled me with incredible emotion which returns each time I hear it.*"

—————⊷❖⊶—————

❧ Memories Revisited ❧

*M*y wife and I attended a marriage enhancement conference called "I Still Do," and I thought it was great that they got Paul Overstreet to play some songs for the conference. When he started singing, "Seein' My Father in Me," I thought to myself, "Oh yeah, that's one of his many songs..." when it hit me like a ton of bricks. My father had just died six weeks previously from complications of lymphoma cancer. For my whole life, everyone I would meet—up to and including at his funeral—would tell me how much I looked like my father. After I became a father of two great kids, I would notice how I used the same phrases he used to tell me. As Paul was singing, it reminded me of how much I missed my dad, and all the emotions came flooding back; I spent the rest of the song sobbing like a baby. I would like to thank Mr. Overstreet for using his God-given abilities for good things, like bringing up some emotions and memories that needed to be vented, aired and revisited every once in awhile.

—**John S.; Cibolo, Texas**

❧ Thanks for the Memories ❧

*T*hanks for the wonderful songs and feelings you have given me over the years. I have listened to "Sowin' Love" probably a thousand times, and it always stays one of my favorites. When I was stationed in Germany, I could only get one American radio station, Armed Forces Network. Once a week, they would play the Country Countdown, and this is where I first heard "Seein' My Father in Me." Hearing this soon after the birth of my first son filled me *with incredible emotion which returns each time I hear it. Each time I see my father in me, now that my son is a teenager and I have another wonderful son. While in Germany, we bought the CD and listened to it almost every night while the three of us ate dinner. You are such a positive songwriter and fantastic artist. Just wanted to say thanks for the memories, and I hope there are more to come.*

—Kevin G.; Dublin, Ohio

❦ Joy Continued ❦

*M*y 83-year old father passed away in 1995, *and your songs were played before his memorial service. "Seein' My Father in Me" was the background music for his video tribute. When my sisters and I were planning our father's memorial, we were looking for just the "right" music with wonderful lyrics and upbeat sounds. We didn't want "funeral" music for our dad's final party!*

When I heard "Seein' My Father in Me" and knew I wanted to use it for the video, I had to buy the entire CD to get that one song. Was I surprised to find that every single song on the CD was just what we were looking for: "Love Helps Those Who Cannot Help Themselves"... "All the Fun"..."Call the Preacher"..."Richest Man on Earth"..."Sowin' Love"..."Love Never Sleeps"..."What God Has Joined Together"...and "'Neath the Light of Your Love" were written with my dad and our family in mind.

Thank you for your music. You'll never know what joy it brought and continues to bring to me whenever I play the CD.

—Vicki R.; Boise, Idaho

"One of the pictures I hold onto when the pain from my past tries to take hold is my Heavenly Father anxiously awaiting me with open arms when I finally get 'home.'"

> "[This] *song is a beautiful way for me to dwell on my relationship with my Heavenly Father.*"

Time for a hug

❧ Healing Song ❧

*T*here are so many of Paul's songs that have touched my heart. "Love Can Build a Bridge" is a song I've sung when my husband and I speak at churches; once I had my students sing it very powerfully while dressed in Native dress. I teach at a Christian boarding school for Navajo and Apache students in Show Low, Arizona. When Paul was in Phoenix one time, I was able to share with him about our work, and it was such an honor to meet him.

Another song that has ministered to me in a very special and unique way is "Seein' My Father in Me." Most people would picture their biological father when they hear this song because obviously that's what it's written about. However, my father sexually abused me from age 3 to 18, and I don't really want to "see him in me." So what I picture is my Heavenly Father in me, and that creates such an awesome feeling. One of the pictures I hold onto when the pain from my past tries to take hold is my Heavenly Father anxiously awaiting me with open arms when I finally get "home."

Another reason this song is powerful in my life is that when I was first in Christian counseling to help me through the worst of the memories, it dawned on me that for all the many years I had been a Christian up to that point, I had **never** prayed, "Dear Father." That song is a beautiful way for me to dwell on my relationship with my Heavenly Father. Thank you, Paul, and may God richly bless you as you have blessed me and so many others.

—**Helen A.**

☜ Great Singer and Humanitarian ☞

I was estranged from my eldest son for some time because of an angry divorce. By accident, I received some mail of his. I was able to contact him...and our differences were resolved. To show he still cared for me, he bought the recording, "Seein' My Father in Me." It brought us closer than ever. He is now married with a great wife and two adopted children from Romania, a boy and a girl. My grandson (from Romania) was born on the same day that I was. We got the children nine years ago, and they are doing just fine.

We have a very good life now. Thanks, Paul; the tape he gave means the world to me, and I still play it often. You are a great singer and humanitarian.

—**Bob D.; New Westminster, British Columbia, Canada**

☜ Meaningful Soul Searching ☞

I was greatly blessed when I heard "Seein' My Father in Me" when I was just out of high school. It was the beginning of some very deep and meaningful soul searching concerning my relationship with my dad. He and my mother were divorced when I was seven, and I held a lot of things against him. It still brings a tear to my eye when I hear or even think about it.

I believe that song has a deep spiritual meaning also, because the greatest thing in my life has been seeing my Heavenly Father in me. I was pleasantly surprised to see that you had written several of my favorite Randy Travis songs as well—I had no idea (and I am not a

"It still brings a tear to my eye when I hear or even think about it."

Cowboy Chord

> *"When I saw your video on this song, I cried along with it, because— while my father is still alive (and well)—this song brought back to me sweet thoughts of my dear mother."*

Country music regular). I thank you for your touching song about fathers and sons, and appreciate how it has touched me.

—**Grant J.**

Seein' Her *Mother* in Her

*I*s there an equivalent to "Seein' My Father in Me" called "Seein' My Mother in Me"? My mother died about ten years ago. I miss her so much, but continue to enjoy great memories of the unique, dynamic person that she was. Everyone tells me that I'm getting more and more like her all the time, and I consider that a compliment, even though she sometimes was "eccentric" (to put it nicely). When I saw your video on this song, I cried along with it, because—while my father is still alive (and well)—this song brought back to me sweet thoughts of my dear mother.

I am comforted to know that—during the last week she was in the hospital—it was our extended family's privilege to fill her room day and night with a cappella *songs of praise and worship…and then we sang her right through those heavenly gates and into the presence of Jesus Christ! I know she'll be waiting with a huge smile on her lovely face when my departure day comes—that's what my father calls "the happiest day of a Christian's life." God bless you for writing this song that ministered so much to me.

—**Joy G.; Grapevine, Texas**

Chapter 3

I Won't Take Less
Than Your Love

I think this song touches on one main truth in this world in which we live: *Love is the greatest treasure you can find.* You can't have happiness or contentment without it. So often in our lives, we have "things"—clothes, jewelry, cars—but they can't fill that emptiness inside us. They might work for a little while…but then you start to feel that need again. So many of us have tried to fill it up with drugs, or drink, or all the toys and possessions we can muster all our days. Love just cannot be replaced. I know—I have tried.

Don Schlitz came by my house one day, and I was amazed when he mentioned the idea of this song to me. I wondered why he would offer me such a great idea. It reminded me of the Bible verse where Jesus said, "Give, and it will be given to you: good measure, pressed down, shaken

Verse One

"How much do I owe you,"

Said the husband
to his wife,

"For standing beside me

Through the hard years
of my life?

Shall I bring you diamonds,

Shall I buy you furs?

Say the word,
and it's yours."

(And the wife said)

Chorus One

"I won't take less than
your love, sweet love;

No, I won't take
less than your love.

All the riches of the world
could never be enough.

I won't take
less than your love."

Verse Two

"How much do I owe you,"

To the mother said the
son,

"For all that you
have taught me

In the days when
I was young?

Shall I bring
expensive blankets

To cast upon your bed,

And a pillow for to
rest your weary head?"

(And the mother said)

together, and running over will be put into your bosom. For with the same measure that you use, it will be measured back to you" (Lk. 6:38). God was blessing me so much. All I know is that I had made a commitment to write songs that I thought God would want me to write—songs that would encourage and bring hope to others...and here was one of the greatest song ideas ever being laid in my lap!

Don and I did write the song, and it was given to Jerry Crutchfield. He told me he knew right away how he wanted to record it. He was producing an album for Tanya Tucker at the time, and had the idea of recording it with her and two guest artists each singing a verse. He wanted Paul Davis, Tanya, and Don Williams to do it. The story I heard was that Don was going to be on vacation in Hawaii during the scheduled recording and would not be able to do it, so they were looking for another artist to make it three. And there I was—kind of like a ballplayer standing on the sidelines yelling, "Put me in, Coach!"—I wanted to be a part of it so badly! However, I was relatively new as a recording artist, so I didn't think I would get a shot at it.

I had also been issued a "letter of suspension" from *MTM Records* after leaving the group *SKO*, which meant I couldn't record for them...and they were certainly not wanting me to record for anybody else. I wasn't sure it could even be worked out. I guess, by the grace of God, I was offered the opportunity. Someone from *Capitol Records* (much smoother than I) was able to work out the details with *MTM*, so I was allowed to sing on the record with Paul Davis and Tanya. I was a huge fan of the great musical gifts that they both had been given, and so making that record was one of my favorite memories.

Paul Davis had just recovered from a near-fatal injury. He had been shot one night in Nashville, and it scared us all. He could have died, but the bullet missed all his vital organs and he recovered slowly; so, for us, to have him sing at all was a miracle. He sang the first verse, which is about a husband talking with his wife…Tanya Tucker sang the second verse, about a mother talking with her son…and I sang the third verse, about a man talking with God, and how God really wants our love more than anything that we can do for Him. In each case, the song says that love is the most important thing we can ever have in our lives.

During that time, I had been wishing that the songs I had been writing would be seen as important to the church, but most of the contemporary Christian music was a lot different from mine. One Sunday, I was sitting in the very back of the church, and a guy got up to address the congregation. He said, "The other day, I was driving down the street, and a song came on the radio. I had been going through a time

Chorus Two

"I won't take less than your love, sweet love;

No, I won't take less than your love.

All the comforts of the world could never be enough;

And I won't take less than your love."

Verse Three

"How much do I owe you,"

Said the man to his Lord,

"For giving me this day,

And every day that's gone before?

Shall I build a temple,

Shall I make a sacrifice?

Tell me, Lord,

And I will pay the price."

(And the Lord said)

Chorus Three

"I won't take less than
your love, sweet love;

No, I won't take
less than your love.

All the treasures of
the world could
never be enough;

And I won't take
less than your love."

"I Won't Take Less Than Your
Love" by Paul Overstreet
and Don Schlitz. Scarlet
Moon Music (BMI)
~ Writers Group Music (BMI)
~ MCA Music
(a Division of MCI, Inc.)
(ASCAP) ~ Don Schlitz Music
(ASCAP). 1986.

when I didn't feel like God really loved me. As the song played, I listened…and became intensely aware of God impressing upon me how much He loved me. It was such a moment that I had to pull off to the side of the road."

Then he asked the sound guy, "Please start the song." I was sitting there in total shock as I heard the song begin: "I Won't Take Less Than Your Love." I won't tell you all that happened to me that day sitting in that church, but I will tell you it was one of the most moving experiences in my life…to know that God, the Creator, was using a song I had been a part of to let His child know that He loved him. At the same time, it was fulfilling a desire in my own heart!

Now that's communication! Skye and Daddy

Letters

—➤•◆◄—

❧ Always Be Thankful ❧

Your song, "I Won't Take Less Than Your Love," with Paul Davis and Tanya Tucker was a very inspirational song to me. It's the type of Christian Country song that most people can identify with. It shows us we should always be thankful to God for everything we have. I pray God will richly bless you with all your future projects.

—**Stephen R.; Rockwood, Tennessee**

❧ Now He Understands ❧

My favorite Paul Overstreet song is "I Won't Take Less Than Your Love." I hear that song and think back to how my parents made sacrifices for me to get through school and the Navy. I never understood why they—or others who have helped me through the years—would not accept some sort of compensation for their efforts, until I read about "God being love" in First John [see 1 Jn. 4:8,16]. Then I would listen to this song, and realize it was all for the love they had for me that enabled them to do the sacrifices without complaining. I finally began to understand that God—or those who loved me—only wanted me to love them in return. I am so thankful for Mr. Overstreet taking the time to help me understand how someone would not take anything less than my love.

—**Jeff W.; Marietta, Georgia**

About Paul Overstreet

Tuning in to Country Music

One night at the movies, he saw *Your Cheatin' Heart*, and was amazed that a man could take a guitar and his gift of singing, and write down what he was feeling and make a living. He knew right then what he would do with his God given gift. Of course, he was side-tracked by sports, but—as he says—he "got over it."

(More about Paul Overstreet in Chapter 4)

—➤•◆◄—

Awards

"Forever and Ever, Amen" *1987 Academy of Country Music Song of the Year*

"I Won't Take Less Than Your Love" was included on the album, **A Songwriter's Project—Volume One**, released in August, 2000, along with these additional songs:

Same Ole Me

When You Say Nothing at All

Forever and Ever, Amen

A Long Line of Love

Diggin' Up Bones

Be Mine

On the Other Hand

I Fell in Love Again Last Night

Toughest Battles

What Are Friends For?

When Mama Ain't Happy

(BMG Music; RCA Corporation)

❧ Grandma's Pies ❧

*W*hen I was growing up, my grandma was very special to me. She would make the best lemon meringue pie; all I had to do was ask. But it was like a game: I'd tell her I'd pay her a million dollars, and she said, "It ain't enough." So I'd say, "I'll give you a kazillion dollars and twelve cents," and she'd say, "Ain't enough." Then we would laugh, and she'd pat my head with flour-coated hands, throw her arms around me and say, "I won't take less than your love! I won't take less than your love!" She'd give me this big hug…and make the lemon meringue pie.

When my grandma died a few years back, I dug out your tape with Tanya Tucker and Paul Davis, and played it all the way to Ohio for the funeral. When I hear that song today, I feel her arms around me and smell the lemon pie baking. Mr. Overstreet, did you realize you were writing such a powerful song? You have helped me keep my grandma close to me long after her death. Thank you very much.

—**Rich M.**

❧ Radio Classic ❧

*W*hen I was a child, I used to hear "I Won't Take Less Than Your Love" on the radio. I didn't know who sang it, but it stuck in my mind all these years. Recently I learned that the singers were Tanya Tucker, Paul Davis, and Paul Overstreet. I believe that song is a true radio classic, for it shows that love—whether between husband and wife, parent and child, or person and God—is more valuable than all the material objects in the world.

—**Collins C.**

Chapter 4

—◆—

A Long Line of Love

On the first Mother's Day after our son, Nash, was born, it hadn't even dawned on me that I should be the one to go out and get a Mother's Day card for my wife. Like a lot of men, I reasoned, "Well, she's not my mother!" So I hadn't done anything special for her, not even on Nash's behalf...and I couldn't figure out why Julie would be so upset, why it even mattered. She couldn't believe that I had forgotten to give her something that recognized that this was her first Mother's Day!

It was a miserable day. We went to church, but we were miserable. At church, they always have all the mothers stand up and they pray for them...but that just made me feel more guilty. So on the way home from church, I stopped by the store to get her a gift...but **now** she didn't want it—it was **too** late, it no longer had any purpose or meaning.

Verse One

I bought a beautiful diamond ring

And offered it to the sweetest thing I know,

And she said that she would take it.

We started making some wedding plans;

She looked at me and took my hand,

And said, "Are you sure we can make it?"

I said, "My Granddad's still in love with my Grandma";

I said, "My Dad still thinks my Mom's the finest thing he ever saw."

Chorus One

"You see, I come from a
long line of love.

When times get hard,
we don't give up.

Forever's in my heart
and in my blood.

You see, I come from a
long line of love."

Verse Two

Years went by,
and we had a son;

Now he thinks that he's
found someone for him,

And they're planning
a wedding.

He called me up
on the phone today,

Just to see what I had
to say to him;

Did I think he
was ready?

I said what his
Grandfather used to
say to me,

"It's been handed
down for ages,

It runs in our family."

After awhile, I had all I could care for, and I took off in the car. I didn't know where I was going and didn't care— I was just getting away. As I was driving along, I turned on the radio for a little music. A song was playing on the radio...and it sounded familiar, so I turned it up to hear what it was. It was the new release by Michael Martin Murphy: "A Long Line of Love"—my song...on the radio! I was thrilled! I started singing along, *"When the times get hard, we don't give up."* Then I thought, "Wow, we wrote that, didn't we! What am I doing?" So I went to the store, got a soda and headed home.

It had really dawned on me: "I need to go back and work this stuff out!" Before this, I had been telling myself that we were writing songs that would make a difference in people's lives, songs that would have a positive impact...but I kept hearing these whispers in my head that I was just kidding myself, my songs were not that important. At that moment, it occurred to me that— if for no other reason— I should keep writing these songs because of what they did for *me* in my marriage. I thank Thom Schuyler for sharing with me in this process.

In all marriages, there are times when you argue, have disagreements. Life isn't perfect, and two people with totally different lives coming together and trying to live as one—there's going to be tension and strife, it's going to be difficult at times. But a good marriage speaks for itself in the long run, and there's victory there. Our kids may see us argue, but at least they know that we still love each other and will work it out.

In some ways, this song really goes with "When Mama Ain't Happy," because they're both about the same thing: how to work it out, and what it's like when it does work out. It used to drive my wife nuts when we'd go out on the road, and women would come up to the autograph table and say, "Gosh, it must be great to be married to him!" And she would say, "Yeah, right." But this *is* what marriage is all about—working out our differences and coming to a middle place that's good.

Chorus Two

"You see, you come from a long line of love.

When times get hard, you won't give up.

Forever's in your heart and in your blood.

You see, you come from a long line of love;

You come from a long line of love."

"A Long Line of Love" by Paul Overstreet and Thom Schuyler. Scarlet Moon Music (BMI) ~ Screen Gems-EMI Music, Inc. (BMI) ~ Bethlehem Music (BMI). 1986.

Paul on stage with the Overstreet gang.
Paul, Harmony, Chord, Summer, and Nash

> *"Thank you for following your heart, your dreams and your God."*

About Paul Overstreet

Tuning in to Country Music *(continued)*

During the days while his mom would do the ironing (and all the other kids were at school), the radio would be tuned in to a Country station...and to Paul, it almost seemed like he could tell what the words were going to be before they were sung. He

Letters

☙ Follow Your Heart ☙

*I*t's been years since I first heard Mr. Overstreet's music. Since then I've had this yearning for songwriting to be a part of my life, especially after finding out that Mr. Overstreet was the writer of the songs that other performers touched my life with growing up. I never had a good family life to look forward to when [I] married and had kids, so the very songs he sings are the sort of vision that I have in raising my children. "Seein' My Father in Me" is exactly the way I want my son to think of me. "Daddy's Come Around"—I know every man can relate to!

But the most beautiful song to me is "A Long Line of Love," for several reasons. The day I asked my wife to marry, we drove up to a mountain where we had our first kiss. I played her that song as sort of a vision statement to the life I was prepared to offer her—that when our kids grew up, they would be able to say that about us. Mr. Overstreet, your music has inspired my life in every way that a role model could. Thank you for following your heart, your dreams and your God. Two years ago, I gave my life to Jesus Christ, and it's great to see someone so close to Music Row who is not afraid to stand up for what is right. Thank you for being you!

— **Daniel U.; Tucson, Arizona**

❧ Honesty ❧

"*A Long Line of Love*" *has always been an inspiring song to me. Even more so now that I've been dating this girl on a steady basis for over two years. The words are so honest and express exactly how I feel. It's kind of like our song. We plan on getting married eventually, and we both want it to last "until death do us part." It is songs like this that keep us inspired, especially through the rough times and through the times when we disagree and have little fights. I have a deep respect for Paul Overstreet; he is truly God-sent and gifted. I pray the Lord will continue to use him to touch other lives.*

— **Mike S.; Rio Hondo, Texas**

❧ Our Song ❧

In 1986, I became a single teenage mother. After my fiancé left me pregnant, I was very hurt and discouraged about the future. I prayed that God would protect and provide for me and the baby I chose to keep, and some day bring her a "special" Daddy who would step up and take care of us both. I didn't date at all for a year after my fiancé left—the pain and betrayal was just too deep. I told God that if He wanted my baby girl to have a Daddy, He'd just have to bring him to us.

In May 1987, I met my soul-mate, sent straight from Heaven. The day I met him, I told my best friend, "I just met the guy I'm going to marry!" She told me I was crazy, but I knew as soon as I looked up into his eyes who he was.

remembers listening to songs by Marty Robbins ("Devil Woman" was his favorite), Charlie Pride, Hank Williams Sr., Jim Reeves, Johnny Horton, Merle Haggard, and, of course, Elvis Presley and Ricky Nelson. As he got older, he listened to a lot of Rock music: the Doobies, Janis Joplin, Three Dog Night, Grand Funk Railroad, Bread. While living in California with his dad for a couple of summers, he learned to play and sing most of Creedence Clearwater Revival's songs. He also always loved R&B—older stuff like Sam Cook, Otis Redding, O.C. Smith, and a lot of Motown.

(More about Paul Overstreet in Chapter 5)

"A Long Line of Love" *was included on the album,* **A Songwriter's Project– Volume One** *released in August, 2000, along with these additional songs:*

Same Ole Me

I Won't Take Less Than Your Love

When You Say Nothing at All

Forever and Ever, Amen

Diggin' Up Bones

Be Mine

On the Other Hand

I Fell in Love Again Last Night

Toughest Battles

What Are Friends For

When Mama Ain't Happy

(BMG Music; RCA Corporation)

Awards

"On the Other Hand" 1987 *Music City News* Traditional Country Song of the Year

One week later, he asked me to marry him; two weeks later, we were married. One month later, he was granted permission to adopt my baby girl. Six weeks after we married, we got pregnant, and had another daughter!

We adopted "A Long Line of Love" as our song when we married. It's been so special to us over the years. We have had hard times when we wondered if we'd make it or not, but we've hung in there because we both come from "A Long Line of Love." We love all of Paul's music. There is such real depth to the lyrics—they touch our hearts deeply.

— **Tammy W.**

∾ Commitment to Faithfulness ∾

*W*hen my husband and I first announced our engagement, I'm sure my mother-in-law (and probably others) had concerns about our ability to have a lasting marriage. Since my parents were divorced and remarried to other people, I didn't exactly have perfect role models. So when I was choosing songs to be played or sung at our wedding, we decided upon the hymn, "Great Is Thy Faithfulness"…the song, "By My Side" (from the musical Godspell)…and Paul Overstreet's song, "A Long Line of Love."

— **Karen C.; El Paso, Texas**

∾ The Promise of the Song ∾

I heard Michael Martin Murphy sing "A Long Line of Love" over the radio in 1987, just *weeks before my wedding. I fell in love with the promise that your lyrics held for the future of a young couple who have a strong love, such as I had for my future husband. I shared the song with my love, and he too felt the promise and we knew that this would be the song to be played at our wedding. His father dedicated the song to us as we held hands beneath the arch, and I could tell that our hearts were unified in sharing the promise of facing the future together.*

It has been 13 years for us, and we have two beautiful daughters. The times have been rough, but my husband still looks upon me with the same eyes, alight with love, and it is a stronger, more lasting love than we knew in our youth. It is the love that your song promised would be born from the years of trial and strength. To this day, my eyes tear up when I hear this song, and I am reminded that my life is complete because of the promise that no matter what we face, we will always face it together!

— LaVerne I.; Pottsville, Arkansas, USA

"There is such real depth to the lyrics— they touch our hearts deeply."

Paul and Julie at a Focus on the Family retreat at Elk Canyon, Colorado

The Overstreet family strolling on the farm

Chapter 5

Love Helps Those Who Cannot Help Themselves

T here is an old saying that I've heard most of my life: "God helps those who help themselves." Years later, I found out that it's not in the Bible. In fact, what the Bible *does* say is: "*With God*, all things are possible" (Mt. 19:26; see also Mk. 9:23) and "I can do all things *through Christ* who strengthens me" (Phil. 4:13). One thing I know for sure is that when I couldn't help myself, God was willing and able to get it done.

There was a time in my life when I was playing around with some of the "recreational" drugs. I could wake up in the morning and get high. At some point, it changed from "play" to something different...the next thing I knew, I couldn't stop. It was probably about a year that I tried to stop on my own. I would wake up in the morning and try to stay straight, and sometimes do okay there. But somewhere during the day, someone would offer drugs,

Verse One

Grandma, she don't really
get around good anymore;

In fact, to get her
out the house

Is really quite a chore.

But every day,
somebody seems to
find the time to stop

To see if Grandma
needs something

From where they
go to shop.

'Cause you see ...

Chorus

Love helps those who
cannot help themselves.

It cares about
those hearts

That's been put up
on a shelf.

It will introduce
a lonely soul

To a lonely someone else.

Love helps those who can-
not help themselves.

Verse Two

Mister Johnson had
a small farm

Down in southern
Tennessee,

But one year, he took ill

Before the time
to plant the seed;

And no one knows which
neighbor planted,

Or they just won't tell,

But he had his
best crop ever

and I'd fall right in there with them. I hated the weakness that I found in myself. I'd go home feeling so defeated.

Then I started praying about it. As time went by, I started waking up early in the morning to read the Bible—and I'd feel great. In the next few minutes, I would think about work and writing, and I'd pick up the guitar. I wouldn't feel that inspired, so I would grab a joint, thinking, "If I take a hit of it, I'll get creative." As soon as I would do that, I'd feel tired and worthless, and just go back to bed. This went on for awhile, but soon I started to realize if I just kept reading the Bible and quit the smoking, I'd just get stronger and stronger. I can't remember the last time I smoked marijuana—the desire just went away.

Then the testing came. I went to a business meeting, with a major record deal on the table. The first thing in that meeting that happened was that a joint was lit and passed around. I was offered some of it, and I refused. To make a long story short, I didn't get the record contract...but I got something better: I got the confirmation, under pressure, that I was finally free of smoking dope!

Sometime later, I was cleaning up around the house, and I heard someone talking on the radio. I thought I heard the phrase, "God helps those who cannot help themselves." I turned the radio up and listened, but soon realized they were nowhere near that kind of conversation. So I grabbed my guitar and started messing around with that phrase. The next thing I knew, I had a song going!

The first verse is about my own grandmother, Minnie Overstreet. She was the mother of 12 children (my dad was the oldest), was widowed in her fifties, loved to fish and laugh, and was quite a character. She died in her own home at the age of 93. Her children always made sure she was taken care of and never alone. The second verse is based on a true story told to me by Mac MacAnnally, who is a great songwriter himself. The last verse is about a fictional young man who meets a girl who is a single mother; he loves both her and her child so much that he accepts them both—that takes a strong individual. This story parallels the Bible story about how Mary became pregnant by the Holy Spirit, and Joseph still loved her and took care of her and the Child—who was Jesus—just like He was his own son.

Letters

✎ Reminded of the Blessings ✎

My parents married young (Mom was 16, Dad was 19) because of me, and divorced when I was 7. I remember my mother not eating, but putting food on the table for me. I remember her falling into bed exhausted after mowing the yard, doing the wash, even changing the spark plugs in her car. "You Can't Stop Love" and "Love Helps Those Who Can't Help Themselves" really hit home for me. We used to go to stores where children were

By the time
that he got well.

'Cause you see ...

Verse Three

A little helpless
baby child

Was born into this world;

She didn't have a Daddy,

And her mother
was just a girl.

But there came a
young man willing

To give both of
them a home;

The girl he married,
the child he cherished

As though she was
his own.

'Cause you see ...

Love Helps Those Who Cannot Help Themselves by Paul Overstreet. Scarlet Moon Music (BMI). 1988.

About Paul Overstreet

Tuning in to Country Music *(continued)*

A man who had been a *Grand Ole Opry* personality was traveling through, and he showed some interest in Paul's music. Paul had pressed three hundred 45's of a demo session he had recorded in Little Rock, Arkansas. The song was called, "The Wanderer." The local Check-A-Sack had agreed to set some by the cash register to see if they would sell. This man, Walter Bailes, bought a copy for one dollar, listened to it ... and contacted Paul. Paul then drove to Tennessee to meet with him. They talked, but never wound up working together. At least it got Paul thinking about Nashville.

(More about Paul Overstreet in Chapter 6)

yelling for toys and asking for things. I didn't do that—I knew, even then, how much it hurt Mom that she wasn't able to give me those things. "Heroes" is also special because that's what Mom is to me—My Hero. I can't listen to those songs without feeling an overwhelming sense of love and respect for my mom. Thanks for reminding me to enjoy the blessings the Lord has bestowed upon us since then.

—Tina F.; Hicksville, Ohio

❧ Strength to Continue ❧

*T*hank you for your wonderful, inspiring music. You are certainly one talented man! My husband courted me on your music. I couldn't remember ever hearing of you before, but I immediately fell in love with your music. There is so much truth found in the words. My favorite song is "Love Helps Those Who Cannot Help Themselves." The entire third verse is my story. When I first heard it, it gave me the strength to continue dating in hopes that I might find a second husband and father for my baby girl. We are now married, with three children. We love your music and the way you have of making everyday feelings make sense. You truly have a great gift!

—Charlotte M.; Mesa, Arizona

❧ The Story of Her Life ❧

*W*hen I was 19, I fell in love and married a young man. He quickly became very abusive, so I left after only nine months of marriage. Twenty days after I left, I found out I was pregnant. I was excited, yet devastated—I'd

always wanted to be a mother. I was also wanting to get remarried sometime in the future,
but I didn't think anyone would want to marry
an instant family. I couldn't understand anyone
willingly choosing that type of life at a time
when you're supposed to be newlyweds. Nine
months later, a new baby girl was born, without a father.

Seven months after my divorce was final, I
met a young man, Kyle, who immediately
showed interest in me, as well as my daughter.
He met her on our first date, and later that
evening, made the comment that whoever
married me would have to marry her too. He
said it with such sincerity that it tenderly
touched my heart. As we dated, Kyle introduced me to the music of Paul Overstreet. He
gave me an old tape, his only copy of the
"Sowin' Love" album, because I fell in love
with a particular song that gave me hope. I listened to the music over and over…I loved the
song "Love Helps Those Who Cannot Help
Themselves," because it described everything
that I felt exactly as I felt it. It also later
became the story of our life.

Kyle was so loving and willing to give both
of us a home. He loves my daughter with
everything in him, as though she were his own.
I've never known a man with more love and
tenderness in him. I owe him and my Father in
Heaven much gratitude and thanks. I try every
day to show my husband how much I love him
and how grateful I am for what he has done
for both of us…and now, our new son.

— **Charlotte M.**

**"Love Helps Those
Who Cannot Help
Themselves"**
was included on the album,
Sowin' Love released in
1989, along with these
additional songs:

All the Fun

Call the Preacher

Richest Man on Earth

Sowin' Love

Love Never Sleeps

Dig Another Well

Seein' My Father in Me

What God Has Joined
Together

Homemaker

'Neath the Light
of Your Love

(BMG Music; RCA Corporation)

Awards
"On the Other Hand"
1987 Country Music
Association
Song of the Year

"Our marriage has lasted 12 years now, with its ups and downs and times of extreme difficulties—but we have made it through and our 'love is strong'! I really appreciate Paul's ability to put Christian messages and principles into his music."

❧ It All Made Sense ❧

"Love Helps Those Who Cannot Help Themselves" was a song that was quite popular when I met my husband in 1987. At that time, I was not a Christian, but he was. I had a little girl almost three years old. The first time my husband and I talked, I gave him a rundown of what my life had been like as a single mother, a party girl, etc. I also indicated to him a desire to change. He accepted that, accepted me, and we began dating. Within a very short time, I could see the difference Christ made in him, as opposed to the men I had been used to dating…and soon I accepted Christ as my Lord and Savior. We decided on a future together, and he accepted my child as his own, adopting her six months into the marriage (the time the law required).

When I hear "Love Helps Those Who Cannot Help Themselves," I can't help but think of it as "our song": "There came a young man willing to give both of them a home…" How much more could a song fit in a relationship such as ours! It was meant for us at exactly the right time, as well as going along with our philosophy that with love—for yourself, for God, for others—your desire should be to help the helpless…not necessarily only those who just choose to do nothing with their lives, but those who truly need and desire to change circumstances and better situations.

Our marriage has lasted 12 years now, with its ups and downs and times of extreme difficulties—but we have made it through and our "love is strong"! I really appreciate Paul's ability to put Christian messages and principles into his music without making it something that would turn off a non-Christian—it all makes sense!

—K.L.M.

Chapter 6

⟹•⟸

All the Fun

This was written as a "peer pressure" song, and it came straight out of real life. Both my co-writer, Taylor Dunn, and I have worked in construction, and the comments from the song that the guys make are accurate. I used to like to hang out in bars, to drink and play pool, and the thought of going home to the same old thing just wasn't very attractive to me then. For a long time I was single, and had all the opportunities to do all the things that I thought would bring happiness. I only had to answer to me...or so I thought. I hung out in the nightclubs, playing music, drinking, and all the things that go along with it. I can honestly say it never lead to anything valuable or productive in my life.

One night I was playing at a club in Columbus, Georgia, sitting on a barstool by the juke box, waiting for our break to be over so we could go play our next set. It

Verse One

Well, the guys that
I work with,
they work real hard

And they like to
have a good time.

At the end of the day,
it's their time to play,

And they like to
go and unwind.

Well, they make
a lot of jokes,

And they laugh and
they poke fun at me

Because I don't
stay long.

And they can't
understand why a
married man

Is in a hurry to
ever go home.

I just tell them that …

Chorus

All the fun that I'm ever
going to need

I got waiting
at home for me.

Yeah, she likes
to dance, and
she loves romance,

And she throws
a great party.

No, there's never any dull
minutes around here,

Something's always
going on.

All the fun that
a man could want

I got waiting for me
at home.

Verse Two

Well, I used to be a fool

was not a life I enjoyed anymore, and I knew I was drinking way too much—even one of the club owners cared enough to tell me that! Sitting right there, I started talking to God. I said, "God, if You'll get me out of these clubs, I'll quit drinking." It was incredible how fast God worked on that!

Within two weeks, I got a call from an old friend who said she knew a publishing company that might be interested in me writing for them. I jumped at the chance, and didn't waste any time getting back to Nashville for a meeting with them. I got the position. It was a no-brainer for me, so to speak. I was sick and tired of the night club scene anyway.

I wish I could say that I kept my end of the bargain as fast as God did…but I didn't. I kept drinking for six more years. Even after I met Julie, I was still drinking—but one night, I acted like a real jerk to her. I realized that the booze was destroying everything in my life that was valuable. The next day, January 1, 1985, I quit drinking (at least, that was the last time I got drunk). Julie and I were married on January 20, 1985, and by the time this song was composed I had been sober for a couple of years. We had two little ones "running all over the house." I learned from firsthand experience that I'd much rather be home with my wife and my kids than hanging out in some nightclub till the wee hours of the morning!

There is this part of the song that says: "She likes to dance, and she loves romance, and she throws a great party." Guys need to realize that their wives are hungering for a good time every now and then. They like to kick up their heels a little bit too. After working hard all day you may want to go home and just collapse. You need to remember that your wife might have been there all day—it's the same scenery, and the same world for her. With you there, it can be a little more pressure, or you can make it a little more fun. *We* set the mood.

Especially as Christians, we need to find time to have fun together. If my wife wants to dance, then I need to find the energy and the time to dance with her! Sometimes the kitchen is the best place in the world for dancing. My wife is a very gregarious person, and she likes to entertain. I don't need to waste my spare time in bars looking for what I already have at home!

Letters

≈ Encouraging Song ≈

*P*aul's song, "All the Fun," is very encouraging. I decided that whomever I marry must be able to sing this song to me, and he must live by it. To think that a man nowadays would look forward to going home to his wife is almost non-existent. But I hope to be that type of wife whom my husband will look forward to coming home to. Every time that I hear this song, I smile and know that there is someone

And a sucker
for a high time,

Any time, night or day.

I had a round-the-clock
smile,

Just call me and I would be
readily on my way.

But to tell you the truth, I
was lonesome and blue,

Praying for a little light
in my life;

Then a miracle came, and
everything changed

And I made that little
woman my wife.

Let me tell you that . . .

Bridge

We got two little kids
calling me Daddy,

Running all over the
house.

When they finally
go to sleep,

Their Mama and me
cuddle, and we snuggle,

And we party
on the couch.

Yeah, I got . . .

"All the Fun"
by Paul Overstreet and Taylor Dunn. Scarlet Moon Music (BMI). 1988.

About Paul Overstreet

The Day It Began

After high school graduation, Paul went to Waco, Texas, for awhile, working as a mechanic on diesel trucks. It didn't take long for him to realize that was not what he wanted to do with the rest of his life. At a concert one night at the local dance hall where he spent his nights and his hard-earned pay ("and I do mean 'hard-earned'"), he sat and watched Tanya Tucker, one of the performers on the show. As he watched, he thought to himself, "I think I can do

out there for me, just waiting to appreciate me, love me, and be with me forever.

—Jennifer J.; Blackshear, Georgia

An Inspiration to Husbands and Fathers

I married my high school sweetheart in February 1985, right out of school. Doug isn't like most! He has never drank, smoked or chewed. He was born into a Christian home, and decided that is how he wanted to raise his family. We are in church every Sunday morning and night, and every Wednesday night, practically every time the doors open. I guess the song, "All the Fun" really reminds me of Doug. There ain't nothing he wouldn't do or give up for me and our three children. He is an ***awesome*** *husband and daddy. He has owned his own construction company ever since we've been married. I guess we've had to struggle a little bit, but he never let anyone know it. He takes care of us. We need a lot more like him! And that part in the song—"After the kids are in bed, their Mama and me, we hug and snuggle and party on the couch"—well, that part is true too. He always takes time to let me know I'm important to him. Thank you, Paul, for your wonderful, "homey," loving songs. They've inspired a lot of men to take time and see what's behind their own front doors.*

—Kristi D.; Louisville, Tennessee

Lyrics Reinterpreted

We discovered Paul's music when we lived in Nashville for two years. Our children were relatively young at the time, but we all enjoyed listening to his music and singing along. The kids used to grab tennis rackets and pretend they were playing guitars. One song that we really liked singing was "All the Fun." In typical little kid fashion, though, the lyrics occasionally got translated through a child's mind. The line "we snuggle and we cuddle and we party on the couch" somehow got reinterpreted to: "we snuggle in a puddle and we potty on the couch." We can never hear that song without chuckling about those wonderful days with our children in Nashville.

—**Clay C.; Monument, Colorado**

❧ An Awesome Celebration ❧

I am a sign language interpreter. I have a deaf sister and many deaf friends. In the summer

that." After the show, he talked to Tanya and got her picture...never realizing he would some day write several songs that she would take to the top of the Country music charts. The next day, he told the company he was working for that he was going to Nashville; they said they would hold his job open for him.

(More about Paul Overstreet in Chapter 7)

Ganging up on Dad is all the fun that a kid could want!

*"**All the Fun**"*
was included on the album,
Sowin' Love *released in*
1989, along with these
additional songs:

Love Helps Those Who
Can't Help Themselves

Call the Preacher

Richest Man on Earth

Sowin' Love

Love Never Sleeps

Dig Another Well

Seein' My Father in Me

What God Has Joined
Together

Homemaker

'Neath the Light
of Your Love

(BMG Music; RCA Corporation)

⎯⎯⎯●⎯⎯⎯

of 1998, my parents celebrated their 50th anniversary and renewed their marriage vows. For the special music, I signed your song, "All the Fun," and dedicated it to my parents. Of course, they loved it, and my daddy cried. It was an awesome celebration and your song seemed to be written especially for my mom and daddy and their marriage. They videotaped me signing that song, and my daddy played it over and over again; he loved it. In December 1998, my daddy went on home to be with the Lord...he graduated. But his anniversary was very special, thanks to your music.

—Liska J.; Oregon

Harmony has fun in the mud!

Chapter 7

Sowin' Love

Don Schlitz and I wrote this song together. In the beginning stages, Don and I used to meet every Monday and Tuesday of every week to write. Some days, we would have an idea to work on before we got to our meeting, sometimes not. One day, Don might have "the idea," the next time maybe I would.

One day, I went into our meeting with an idea for a song called "Sowin' Love"—about the "seeds of love" that we sow throughout our lives—but when I mentioned the title to Don, he looked at me kind of perplexed. He said, "I think we can find something stronger than 'so in love' to write about. It's so over-used!" Well, he was right—"so in love" *is* a very over-used expression. But I as clarified it for him—that I was meaning "sowing love," like "you reap what you sow"—he began to get it.

Verse One

I used to love to walk behind my Daddy

As he plowed our garden every spring;

My little bare feet in the dirt would make me happy,

As we talked about what harvest-time would bring.

He'd say, "Son, this whole world is like a garden,

And what you sow, you're surely going to reap.

Where bitter seeds are planted, hearts will harden;

But a caring hand will make the harvest sweet."

Chorus One

He was sowing love
for the family.

He was sowing love,
he took a little extra time;

Looking forward to a
bountiful harvest.

Like a good father does,
he was sowing love.

Verse Two

How I used to love to sit
and watch my Mama

Working with her
needle and her thread;

So patiently, she'd listen
to our problems,

And we knew she heard
every word we said.

She'd say, "Children,
this old world is full
of scratches,

And in your life, you're
bound to have a few;

I guess that's why the good
Lord gave us patches,

So we could start each day
out feeling new."

When I was I kid, I grew up in the country and my dad used to plough this little piece of ground every spring (this was before my parents divorced). I used to walk barefoot behind him, feeling that soft Mississippi dirt just collapsing under my feet. It was a very rich land, and a very sweet time in my life. That experience made an impact on me…you just don't forget those kinds of things.

Don and I talked awhile about sowing the seeds of love. Then we took it to another idea, using a different spelling of the word, about a mother sewing. I remembered watching my own mother sit at her sewing machine for hours during the day, and how we used to talk then. I'm sure a lot of folks can relate to the mother in this song—how her kids were watching her sew, and how she was talking with her kids while she worked on their behalf. She was also listening to them, to the things that interested or puzzled them. Even while her hands were busy sewing, she was showing how much she loved them and cared for them, just by listening while she worked.

Don is a real artist with lyrics. He can paint such a beautiful picture with a phrase. After the "sewing love" verse, the song then migrated to the more simple "so in love" verse. And this is really important—and is sometimes difficult for young people to understand—that true love outlasts "physical attraction"…but it can certainly last a lifetime. The marriages I've seen where the husband and wife were so in love—everything else revolved around that. In this song, that's why this couple did all the other "sowing" and "sewing"—because they were "so in love"!

I have a huge respect for Don Schlitz. He has an ability to take an idea, open it up, and get more out of it than you can ever think possible. I will always be thankful for the many songs we wrote together, and the many days we spent just talking about life and different philosophies. I have been so blessed to work with Don, and to sing the lyrics to the songs that we wrote together, night after night, performance after performance. I never get tired of a great song with a great meaning. I like to think that a song like this will still mean as much 20 years from now as it did on the day of its first release.

Letters

≈ Life Experiences in Overstreet Songs ≈

I see so many of my own experiences in the lyrics of Paul Overstreet's songs that it is difficult to pick just one that has affected my life. Coming from a large, economically poor farm family in a rural southern Indiana farm

Chorus Two

She was sewing love
for the family.

She was sewing love;
she took a little extra time;

Looking forward to a
bountiful harvest.

Like a good Mama does,
she was sewing love.

Chorus Three

Yeah, they were so in love
for the family.

They were so in love;
they took a little
extra time;

Looking forward to a
bountiful harvest.

They took good care of us,
they were so in love.

They did it all for us, they
were sowing love.

"Sowin' Love"
by Paul Overstreet and
Don Schlitz. Screen Gems-
EMI Music, Inc.
Scarlet Moon Music (BMI)
MCA Music Publishing
(a Division of MCA, Inc.)
Don Schlitz Music (ASCAP).
1988.

About Paul Overstreet

Off to Nashville

Paul came to Nashville driving a 1968 Ford Fairlane given to him by his brother Wiley. Not owning a suitcase, he brought with him a laundry basket of Levis and football jerseys, ten original songs, and a guitar. He packed them in the car with a lot of dreams about how great it was all going to be when he finally got to the "big city." A friend came with him, and between the two of them, they had about two hundred dollars (which lasted about a week and a half). Paul didn't have a clue what to do next...but he was there!

(More about Paul Overstreet in Chapter 8)

community, I find myself relating to so many of Paul's songs. Our family was brought up going to the small country church about a mile from our home. In church we learned morals, the way to salvation, and the way God wanted us to live. At home, we saw those lessons reinforced. It's apparent from listening to Overstreet's songs that these are the kind of values he also holds dear.

My father died in January 1999. I live about half an hour away from my mother and the old family homestead. My wife, children, and I go there often. I miss my father when I go there...I think about my dad, and how I too "used to love to walk behind my Daddy as he plowed our garden every spring." What a garden it always was, right up until he kept his last garden at the age of 81. He and my mom were definitely "sowing love."

I also think about how poor my seven brothers and sisters were, not having nearly as much as our peers, who no doubt made fun of our station in life. But I also know how my parents worked every day so we'd have everything we need. I realized...that there was "a roof over our heads, the kids had all been fed, and the woman my dad loved most was right beside him in the bed." [from the song "Richest Man on Earth."]

My parents demonstrated a kind of love, loyalty and commitment that is becoming too rare...I learned from their sterling examples what it takes to make a marriage work. It means putting up with a few faults, knowing there will be struggles, and caring more about your partner than you care about yourself. This is what I needed to know because someday, I would have a family of my own.

My wife and I have daughters who are 11 and 14. There are bills to pay, but I also know that if only I think of it, as such I am the "richest man on Earth." My wife is a wonderful blessing. In raising a family, there are many demands I must meet so I can provide for my family. There's a little bit of my experiences in every Paul Overstreet song I hear.

—**Roger M.**

Redheads stick together

"I think about my dad, and how I too 'used to love to walk behind my Daddy as he plowed our garden every spring.' What a garden it always was, right up until he kept his last garden at the age of 81."

"Sowin' Love"
was included on the album,
Sowin' Love released in
1989, along with these
additional songs:

Love Helps Those Who
Cannot Help Themselves

All the Fun

Call the Preacher

Richest Man on Earth

Love Never Sleeps

Dig Another Well

Seein' My Father in Me

What God Has Joined
Together

Homemaker

'Neath the Light
of Your Love

(BMG Music; RCA Corporation)

———⟫•❂•⟪———

Awards
"On the Other Hand"
1987 *Music City News*
Traditional Country
Song of the Year

☙ Captures Life ❧

*T*his is possibly one of the cleverest Country
songs I've ever heard, with its three distinct
uses of "sowing love"…"sewing love"…and "so
in love." But once you get past how clever is the
song, you also realize how true it is. The fundamental relationship in life is between parent and
child—whether we're talking about God and His
children, or human beings—and is one where
love is the essential ingredient. Mr. Overstreet
has captured life perfectly, and with wisdom, in
his music. Thank you!

—John M.; Miami, Oklahoma

☙ Wholesome Encouragement ❧

I have all of your tapes and introduce you to
my friends because we appreciate the wholesome, encouraging messages in your songs.
When I first heard "Sowin' Love," I thought, "I
have to get that and play it around my children!" I wanted them to hear the care of the
parents for the family, and the appreciation of
the husband for his wife. I have shared your
music with teenagers on long church camp
road-trips, and they love them too.

Not only do I appreciate the direction in
your songs, but I like the sound of your music—
I find it a lot of fun! Once I had a young man
riding with me in the car who wasn't too sure
about this "Christianity stuff." I put on one of
your tapes, and he said, "Hey, this is alright!"
Thanks, Paul, for good and wholesome music to
feed our souls, and help to point us and our families in a godly direction.

—Carol H.

✎ Best Friend Forever ✎

The second verse of "Sowin' Love" means a lot to me. I cried when I first heard it because I grew up very poor. As a matter of fact, we lived in a broken-down building on someone else's property; it was originally built to be an apple barn. We had no indoor bathroom facilities, no hot running water, and only a small wood-burning stove for heat. My father was an alcoholic, so he wasn't around much, and when he was, he was abusive. But my mom was there for us all the time. We knew she was hurting, but she always listened to our heartache and tried to comfort us.

She was then—and is now, and always will be—my best friend. The love she sowed there kept me alive at that time, and because she always pointed us to the Lord, one day I heard and understood the extent of His love for me. I knew where she got the strength to love us and continue with life until the Lord would deliver her. I always wished for a relationship with my dad like the one in the song.

I think kids have an automatic sense of love and admiration for their parents, no matter how unworthy we are as parents. As I look back, I remember the way I felt for my dad, and I know that even though he is gone now, our relationship is healed. Thank God he accepted the Lord before his death, and even had a few years to tell us how sorry he was. In my heart, I can have that relationship with him, and I know "harvest time will bring" us together again, to be together for eternity, and

"I think kids have an automatic sense of love and admiration for their parents, no matter how unworthy we are as parents. As I look back, I remember the way I felt for my dad, and I know that even though he is gone now, our relationship is healed."

"Thanks, Paul, for good and wholesome music to feed our souls, and help to point us and our families in a godly direction."

we will have that loving relationship we should have had all along.

—Judy C.

≈ Kept Close in "Desert Shield" ≈

I had heard Paul's music sometime prior to 1990, and it was entertaining, heartfelt Christian music—yet it was good Country music that anyone could enjoy. In October 1990, several of we airmen from the 94th Maintenance Squadron volunteered to go to the Middle East as part of Desert Shield. Many nights I lay in my bunk and listened to Paul's "Sowin' Love." It encouraged me to pray for my family back home, and it moved me to be thankful for the blessing of a wonderful wife and beautiful children. I was thankful for the music of Paul Overstreet because it kept me close to home when I was so far away.

—**Lester W.; Marietta, Georgia**

Chapter 8

Dig Another Well

When I was in a Bible Study Fellowship, we were studying the Book of Genesis. I read where Isaac, the son of Abraham, was having a lot of trouble with his neighbors. For one thing, there was a famine in the land and things were not going so well for them. Isaac was living right next to them, camped around a well that his father Abraham had dug. The Bible says that the Lord was blessing Isaac a hundred-fold.

Now that would tend to make some people more than a little uneasy. They were seeing the favor of God on one of God's own, and their jealousy raged. They began to come out in the middle of the night and fill up Isaac's wells with dirt and rocks. Water was like gold in those days. That was enough to justify going to war over, but instead of choosing that, Isaac just moved a little farther away and dug another well.

Verse One

Well, Ike had a blessing
from the Lord up above,

He gave him a beautiful
woman to love,

A place to live and
some land to farm,

Two good legs and
two good arms.

Well, the devil came
sneaking around
one night,

Decided he would
do a little evil to Ike;

Figured he would hit old
Ike where it hurt,

So he filled up all of
Ike's wells with dirt.

When Ike went out for
his morning drink,

Got a dipper full of dirt,
and his heart did sink.

Ike knew it was the devil,
so he said with a grin,

"God blessed me once,
and He can do it again.

He blessed me once,
and He can do it again."

Chorus

So when the rains don't
fall, and the crops all fail,

And the cow's not putting
any milk in the pail;

Don't sit around waiting
for a check in the mail,

Just pick up the shovel,
and dig another well.

Pick up the shovel,
and dig another well.

Verse Two

Me and old Ike
got a lot in common;

The Lord blessed me with
a beautiful woman,

They came out again and did the same thing to the new wells. By that time, I think a lot of us would have been in a mood to remove a few of them from the earth! I'm sure Isaac was too…but once again, he chose a different path. He moved his people and dug another well. Finally, the people of that city left them alone and Isaac said, "Now the Lord has made room for us" (Gen. 26:22b).

This story really started speaking to me because at the time we were studying this, I was also dealing with a lawsuit involving one of our songs, and it was becoming very hard to be kind! (This sort of thing happens all the time in the music industry—as I'm sure in many other industries—but it had never happened before to me!) Don and I always spent time just talking before we wrote, and as I shared some of this with him, he suggested we write about it. What a way to "dig another well" for myself! We wrote about it in this song…and it wasn't long after that that we wrote another song that would become a huge Grammy-award winning song for Randy Travis, "Forever and Ever, Amen." Now there's a nice "well" from God! I took a lesson from Isaac—Don and I nicknamed him "Ike" in the song, since "Isaac" just didn't sound right in a country song (not in this one, anyway).

I believe it's better to focus on positive things and move forward, than allow all your attention and energy to be wasted and misdirected by negative things.

Letters

>—————⟫•⟪—————

⤷ Out of the Dark Times ⤶

I sit here at my computer listening to "Dig Another Well," and tears of remembrance are finding their way down my face. In the summer of 1995, I—along with a few friends—were facing dark times. We were breaking free from a religious cult, and it was nearly breaking us. I didn't think I could go on. All my friends and family were in this cult I was leaving. I thought I had no friends anymore. The leaders of this cult were trashing me with some of the most horrible, false rumors you can imagine…stuff like I was a child molester. I thought I had nothing to live for anymore.

During this time, one of our number brought home a Paul Overstreet tape (having any kind of music was against the rules, and so we had to hide it) with "Dig Another Well" on it. As we were listening to it, we all just cried and cried. It was like a confirmation from God that everything was going to be alright.

Since then, I went from homeless and nearly friendless, to having a beautiful wife and a precious son. Tina, my wife, was part of that group who found freedom. My new friends are ten times better than the old ones I had. That song has become the theme for our lives. Times haven't always been easy, but we will just dig another well. I have dedicated my life to helping my friends in similar situations to "dig another

He gave me a job,
He gave me a home,

He gave me a well
to call my own.

When I go out for
my morning drink,

Get a dipper full of dirt,
and my heart does sink;

But I think of old Ike,
and I have to grin,

'Cause God blessed me
once, and He can
do it again.

He blessed me once, and
He can do it again.

Tag

Well, the Good Book says
Ike finally won

(Pick up the shovel,
and dig another well)

The devil got tired,
and he left him alone

(Pick up the shovel,
and dig another well)

I know some day
I'm going to win too

(Pick up the shovel,
and dig another well)

Pick up the shovel,
and dig another well

(Pick up the shovel,
and dig another well).

"Dig Another Well"
by Paul Overstreet
and Don Schlitz.
Scarlet Moon Music (BMI)
1988.

About Paul Overstreet

A Dream Road With God by His Side

A long, hard road lay ahead, but the dream of writing songs and making records was so big that the roughest roads weren't going to stop him. After sleeping in his car and eating potato salad sandwiches for awhile, he got a job in a water-heater factory. The future was not looking so bright, but somehow the dream stayed alive. Looking back on these early years,

well." I am working towards buying a small farm for them to come to for a few months, to learn the truth about God and how much He loves us. It will be a time of emotional rest since I remember what a near-nervous breakdown feels like. Paul, thank you for helping me when I was at the bottom. I will never forget it. God bless you!

—**Richard M.; Poteau, Oklahoma**

❧ He Was Like Ike ❧

*T*wenty-five years ago, I got my left arm caught in a corn picker. From the beginning, I blamed no one but myself for my foolishness. I taught myself to do everything I was able to do before the accident happened. Some tasks take longer to do. Some minor things I can't do, but I don't let that bother me. The song, "Dig Another Well," sums up my feelings. My accident was allowed by God for my good, so I dug another well. I am like "Ike": God blessed me with a wonderful wife, six children, ten grandchildren, and one great-grandson; the ability to work, play and enjoy life; but most of all, He drew me closer to Himself when I wasn't walking with Him. Through it all, God will be glorified in all that happens in our lives. May God bless you and your family in your ministry.

—**Richard A.**

❧ When Everything Seemed to Be Falling Apart ... ❧

*M*y husband, Jesse, and I have four boys. In 1994, we had our third child; two weeks after he was born, we found out Dillon had four heart defects and was in congestive heart failure. He had surgery when he was six months old. In the midst of difficult times for our marriage and worried about our child, your music lifted our spirits. One special song that comes to mind is "Dig Another Well." When everything seems to be falling apart, just look to God for help and don't let the devil get hold of the situation.

Our son is now five years old and is doing wonderfully. Also my husband plays the guitar, and I love to hear him sing, especially your song about "all the fun that a man could want, I got waiting at home for me." We are much closer now. We both love music, especially yours, because we all love the Lord so much and we thank Him every day for people like you and for all the blessings He has given our family. God bless you.

—**Lynette L.; Albuquerque, New Mexico**

Paul said, "It's amazing to realize that the reality is greater than the dreams that started the whole adventure." Paul is the first to say that it was his talent and vision—given to him by God—that enabled him to reach his goals as a songwriter, artist, and producer.

(More about Paul Overstreet in Chapter 9)

Paul sings and encourages all to "pick up the shovel and dig another well."

> *"In the midst of difficult times for our marriage and worried about our child, your music lifted our spirits."*

> *"[One] thing I learned from the song is to be grateful for what God has given me in life."*

✎ Just Sing a Few Lines … ✎

*W*e all have days when things just don't go our way, but sometimes it seems like everybody and everything is working against us. I was having one of those days when I first heard "Dig Another Well." I realized as I listened to this song that being discouraged, feeling sorry for myself, or just waiting for it to all go away wasn't going to get me anywhere—it was up to me to do something about my situation. And I did! It has been a few years since that day, and I still love that song. In fact, every time I feel like my well has been filled up with dirt, all I have to do is sing a few lines, and I'm ready to go dig another well. Thanks, Paul, for writing this and all of your other songs; they have truly inspired me to be a better, happier person who relies on the Lord more.

—Justin M.

✎ A Tingling Sensation ✎

I can't tell you how much I love your songs. I can only tell you that they touch my soul and leave me with a tingling sensation. It's amazing how much talent God has given you and how He uses you. I am 15 years old, holding my breath until 16 comes around. I love Country music. I first heard of you when my dad put your CD in. I totally loved it, so does my dad. You're my favorite. You come before George Strait. I was wondering if you have your songs in a book so that if I wanted to, I could play them on a guitar and sing. [The themes of] some of the songs you sing have happened *[to my family]*. The devil has come and tried to destroy our family. Like one of your songs says, "I'm going to dig another well." My dad is selling our company to another company...God has provided us a way out of bankruptcy. It reminds me of the "Richest Man on Earth." I love your songs so much, and I am so glad to have heard them. You have a gift, and I am blessed for it. I am a writer; I love to write poems and stories. God told my pastor that I have a calling on my life. Just like you, I will minister to others. May God bless you more in the future and bless others.

—**Heather T.**

⪜ Words of Inspiration ⪜

*T*he song, "Dig Another Well," is so very special to me. It inspired me not only in my early twenties to keep on without losing faith, but it taught me a valuable lesson every child needs to hear: with the Lord's help, anything is possible...and when things go wrong, we keep trying. To be successful in life, we have to keep trying.

The other thing I learned from the song is to be grateful for what God has given me in life. It's not always easy to do, but I am grateful for everything I have. I wish to share Paul's music among our young children, so that if they are feeling down, they will hear words of inspiration to pick them up. We need God's blessings today and every day.

—**James W.**

"Dig Another Well" was included on the album, **Sowin' Love** released in 1989, along with these additional songs:

Love Helps Those Who Cannot Help Themselves

All the Fun

Call the Preacher

Richest Man on Earth

Sowin' Love

Love Never Sleeps

Seein' My Father in Me

What God Has Joined Together

Homemaker

'Neath the Light of Your Love

(BMG Music; RCA Corporation)

Awards
"Forever and Ever, Amen" 1988 *Grammy* (National Association of Recording Arts and Sciences)

"I realized as I listened to this song that being discouraged, feeling sorry for myself, or just waiting for it to all go away wasn't going to get me anywhere—it was up to me to do something about my situation. And I did!"

❧ Literally Another Well ❧

I love your song, "Dig Another Well." It has been uplifting and an inspiration to me. Whenever things around my life are not going really well, I think of that song, and then look for other resources. When the city water line broke in January 2000—with a temperature of 20 degrees [Fahrenheit] outside and one inch of snow on the ground—we had no way of watering our cows. So your song came to mind…and then I remembered the old well on our place. I went out and got water by buckets and chain, the whole time singing your song. So you see, this song has a literal as well as a figurative meaning to me.

My little boy, William (age seven), says to tell you, "I love your singing." I am so glad to hear someone sing who is as talented as you. Keep up the good work.

—Laura R.; Kentucky

Riding lessons from Mom—
Julie and Summer

Chapter 9

———◆———

Richest Man on Earth

I used to hear "scary stories" from music artists who had been successful before I had the chance to walk in those shoes. They often remarked how it happened that they would be gone on the road so much, that one day they would come home and find that their kids were all grown up. This show business "fact of life" was perfectly described in the hit song by Harry Chapin, "Cat's in the Cradle." The basic idea in this song is that a child keeps asking his father to play with him, but the dad is always too busy; then one day, when the dad thinks he finally has time for his son, he discovers that the boy has grown up and gone. It is a very sad song.

That concept stuck somewhere in the back of my mind when I went to the hospital with my wife, who was having an emergency Caesarian section delivery of our first child. Not knowing what to

Verse One

I've heard tell of
millionaires

And billionaires and such

Who gathered
all their treasures

And still did not
have enough.

If money could buy
peace of mind,

I guess they'd have it all;

But all the money
in the world

Won't hold you
when you fall.

Chorus

We've got a roof
over our heads,

And the kids have
all been fed,

And the woman I love most

Lies close beside me
in our bed.

Lord, give me the
eyes to see

Exactly what it's worth,

And I will be the richest
man on Earth.

Verse Two

Lord, when I wish
I had the things

That You gave
someone else,

I pray that
You'll forgive me

For just thinking of myself.

I haven't been
as thankful as

I know I ought to be;

I should be
more than satisfied

With all You've given me.

expect, I was nervously pacing the floor outside the delivery room, trying to come up with some "leverage" to use with God—sort of like, "If I can find something good that I have done for Him, then I can expect Him to help us out in this situation." (Of course, it doesn't work that way...and I couldn't find anything anyway.)

I was "at the end of my rope"...when I remembered the prayer of the man in the Bible: "God, be merciful to me a sinner!" (Lk. 18:13b) I cried that prayer out to God...and when I finished that prayer, I felt a sense of peace come over me. Then I went into the delivery room and held Julie's hand as she gave birth. Julie was fine, and the baby—our first son, Nash—was healthy and doing fine. I knew I had experienced the grace of God in my life. If you had known me before I surrendered my life to God, you would have known why I didn't feel that I was deserving of the great blessings God had given me...but I was so thankful that He had!

As I held my son in my arms there in the delivery room, I heard music begin to play over the speakers—"Cat's in the Cradle." (I later asked if someone had purposely played that song because I knew it was a message for me—but they said it was just what was on the radio.) What a moment! I knew God was speaking to me, and I sincerely said, "Yes, God, I hear You."

I decided that I was not going to let this principle slip by me, that I was going to be there for *all* the stages of my children's lives. That's one of the reasons that

I never toured like a lot of artists do. It was so hard for me to leave for long periods of time—I just couldn't miss my kids growing up! I guess that's why I love songwriting so much, because it allows me to stay close and be around the kids, watching all the things they can do. It's worth it. (For several years, we traveled with the kids in tow, but that got a little hard to do after our family grew to the size it is now—what started out as a "threesome" has grown to an "eightsome"!)

Recently, I was driving down the road and talking with a friend who is working on his music career. Sometimes he feels frustrated and anxious, just like a lot of us. We talked about learning to be happy with what you have, being thankful for the many blessings God gives us daily. It takes all the parts of a dream to make the whole worth having...and if we miss the first part—the days when it doesn't seem like we're getting anywhere—then we will have missed the most important part. Sometimes it's the climb *up* the mountain that is the best. Once we're standing on the top, we wonder what all the worry and fuss was about.

I may not remember what was the actual original inspiration for this song—but I always get a new perspective when I contemplate these lyrics. We live in a fast-moving world. I don't know where we are all in such a hurry to go, but I know that when I slow down and start to look at things through the eyes of humility, I see the truth: at the end of the day, our loved ones are what really matters most.

Tag

One thing is for certain:

It don't matter
when you die

If you had a million,

Or if you just got by.

"Richest Man on Earth" by Paul Overstreet and Don Schlitz. Scarlet Moon Music (BMI) ~ Writers Group Music (BMI) ~ MCA Music (a Division of MCA, Inc.) (ASCAP) ~ Don Schlitz Music (ASCAP). 1988.

About Paul Overstreet

Launching a Career

As a songwriter, Paul Overstreet has written or co-written 27 Top Ten songs, his first being George Jones' "Same Ole Me." Numerous other artists have recorded his songs, including Randy Travis singing "On the Other Hand," "Diggin' Up Bones" and "Forever and Ever,

Amen," and "Deeper Than the Holler." Tanya Tucker topped the charts with "One Love at a Time" and "My Arms Stay Open All Night," and then teamed up with Paul Davis and Overstreet for the hit, "I Won't Take Less Than Your Love." The late Keith Whitley recorded "When You Say Nothing at All"...then Alison Krause took the same song to the top of the charts a second time in 2000.

(More about Paul Overstreet in Chapter 10)

Letters

✎ One Magic Morning ✎

I am a real estate broker who has been very blessed in my life with great customers, friends and working environments. But in 1986, things were really, really bad in the real estate business in Dallas. If you "been to the mountaintops" as I had, things seemed even worse than they probably really were. I spent a lot of time beating up on myself for my stupidity at spending all of the money I had made and at my inability to replace that money, to the point of obsessing about it and wishing fervently that I could stop the world and get off. This was my favorite pastime most of the day, starting when I woke up at 6:00 a.m. listening to the radio.

One magic morning, I heard someone I have never heard before sing a song about the richest man on Earth. I really can't tell you how profoundly I embraced that song because, after hearing it, I recognized that it was written specifically for me. My life got better that morning; not in material ways, but in a realization that I really was "the richest man on Earth" with all the blessings—except money—that a person could ever want. I got into a Bible study group, bought the "Sowin' Love" album, realized I needed to get started "digging another well," and got busy doing so. I realized soon after that what I needed to do was the things Paul—the biblical Paul—tells us in Philippians 4:4-9.

I have since that time given "Sowin' Love" to a number of friends in tight spots. It always ends up helping. I want you to know there is at least one person who thanks God for your talent and your help. You literally saved my life.

—**Jerry S., Dallas, Texas**

❧ Helped Teach His Kids ❧

"*The Richest Man on Earth" is one of the prettiest songs I have ever heard. I consider myself to be the richest man on Earth because of my heart and values. I play the song, which I love very much. I used to sing it to my kids, to try to get them to understand that there is much more about being a rich person than just money.*

—**Tommy G.**

"I love your songs so much, and I am so glad to have heard them. You have a gift, and I am blessed for it."

The Overstreet treasure chest - 1993

"Richest Man on Earth" was included on the album, **Sowin' Love** *released in 1989, along with these additional songs:*

Love Helps Those Who Cannot Help Themselves

All the Fun

Call the Preacher

Sowin' Love

Love Never Sleeps

Dig Another Well

Seein' My Father in Me

What God Has Joined Together

Homemaker

'Neath the Light of Your Love

(BMG Music; RCA Corporation)

Awards

"Forever and Ever, Amen" 1988 *Grammy* (National Association of Recording Arts and Sciences)

⬳ Brazilian Fan ⬲

I am a Brazilian Christian (regular Baptist) who knew your songs on a radio program. I was encouraged by the fact that in the U.S.A., many singers like you have very good quality music with Christian lyrics. I show your songs to many friends. The song I prefer is "The Richest Man on Earth." Last year, many Americans came to my country of Brazil from the state of West Virginia, and I showed to them many of your songs. I apologize for my bad English, but it is the best I can do. I like the Ricky Skaggs songs too. God bless you in your ministry.

—**Ricardo O.; Novo Hamburgo, Rio Grande do Sul, Brazil**

⬳ Defined What Is Important ⬲

*E*ven as a born-again Christian, I had struggles in my life, in particular with alcohol. Through the prayers and patience of my wife and others, I was able to completely overcome this sin, with the Lord's help. This song became popular at that time and was one that allowed me to define as much of what is important to me.

In 1992, my dear wife was called home at age 39, due to a brain tumor. Fortunately, we had some good, sober, Spirit-filled years together. After I had sobered up, I finally realized I was already "the richest man on Earth." This song will always remain an important reminder of what is important in my life, as well as of a simpler, less complicated time in *life for myself and children. Thank you and God bless you.*

—**Steve F.; Columbus, Ohio**

❧ Sustained Through Difficult Times ❧

I've had the Sowin' Love *CD for years, and I still listen to it often. It's such an important tribute to family love and God's love. You hit so exactly on what is really important in life. I have a dear friend whose husband recently lost a high-powered job and their family was forced to drastically change their lifestyle. I could see my friend more and more depressed and hopeless, so one day I bought your CD for her and insisted that she listen to "The Richest Man on Earth" and "Dig Another Well" until she knew them by heart. Since that day, their lives have improved. He got another good job and they are getting back on their feet. She told me the other day that she has listened to that CD many times and it has helped to sustain her through the difficult times. Thanks for helping me encourage and support someone whom I love very much.*

—**Kerrie S.**

❧ A Very Blessed Woman ❧

*I enjoyed the songs from the radio like "Sowin' Love" when I was a teenager, so I bought the tape. It changed my life! My family was a dysfunctional one (I wonder now if there are **any** functional ones!), and I never knew Jesus in a personal way. I moved several*

"This song will always remain an important reminder of what is important in my life, as well as of a simpler, less complicated time in life for myself and children."

> *"When things don't go right, I think of this song... and it puts things back in place."*

Everyone loves a visit from Grandma

times, and my last move was over a thousand miles. Through it all, I lost many things, but my "Sowin' Love" tape stayed with me. As I attended church after my first son was born, I learned to be a better wife and mother from the song, "Homemaker"—it made me want to be all I could for my baby boy. The lyrics in "The Richest Man on Earth" are for me too—"a roof over our head" reminded me to be thankful for our one-bedroom home without air conditioning in Florida.

I have to admit I think [that] Mrs. Overstreet is a very blessed woman—but she would have to be a strong, loving person to generate the love in her husband's songs. Recently, I decided to write a fiction book on a homeless man. I plan to write an acknowledgment to Paul for the song, "There but for the Grace of God Go I." Before I heard that, I used to be hardened to the plight of those less fortunate.

—**Trish A.; Bradenton, Florida**

≈ Thanksgiving ≈

*I*t was Thanksgiving time a few years back, and I felt my children weren't being thankful enough. I had complained about it to a friend, and we spent some time comparing stories. Later that week, I heard "The Richest Man on Earth," and I realized that I was not being thankful enough. That song showed me how rich I am! It is my favorite song. When things don't go right, I think of this song...and it puts things back in place.

—**Tracy E.**

Chapter 10

—=▶◆◀=—

(She Wants to Be a) Homemaker

This song was never a hit single, but it seems to have meant a lot to many women (and men as well). I also learned a lot with this song. The thought came to me back when I was a staff writer for a publishing company on Music Row here in Nashville. I would see a lot of different people in their work environment during the day, taking a minute here and there to catch up with old acquaintances. I started to hear a familiar theme. Some girls said they liked their jobs okay…but they would rather be married, have children, and stay at home with them. I didn't really think that was unusual at all…but like I said, I learned a lot with this song!

When I told my co-writer, Dan Tyler, about my idea, he was willing to write it with me…but he advised caution. When I was curious about that, he began to

Verse One

To me she is a
beauty queen;

I love to watch her
on screen in our
home movies.

And when she sings
around the house,

She's got a voice that
knocks me out;

She is my favorite singer.

But you won't see her
on TV,

Or hear her on the radio;

Worldly fame is not
her aim,

And she's the first
to let you know.

Chorus

She wants to be
a homemaker.

It's her dream to
raise a family,

And to give her heart
to just one man;

And I thank God it's me.

And I'll never
underestimate her,

'Cause she could take
the world and turn it on;

But she takes her love,

And makes our
house a home.

Verse Two

Can't afford to
spend her days

In an old soap opera haze;

She's much too busy.

At night, she puts the
kids in bed,

She's making sure their
prayers get said,

Before she lays
down with me.

explain that it might be a little controversial. I still didn't see what all the worry was about—besides, I had married a girl who was the perfect example for the song! So we pushed on ahead and wrote it.

After the song was recorded, the producer, some of the record company staff and executives, and I were listening to the playback of some of the mixes, trying to decide which song would be the single. We played the mix of that song, and I thought it was great. When I was asked which song I would like for a single, I mentioned "Homemaker." One of the women from the record company advised against it right away. When I asked why, she said, "Because I don't want women to hate you!"

The reality of the conflict became a little clearer to me at that point. I've learned a lot more about this issue since then. There were some interviews where a female would take offense with the song...but all in all, it's been mild. To hear the expressed comfort that some women have found just resting in the truth that it's right for them to have that desire in their hearts (to be a stay-at-home wife and mother)—and to embrace it—that is worth it. It's not that the homemaker doesn't have anything else going on in her life. Her dream is not to please society, but to make society a better place because she has raised children and made a home. (By "raised," I mean really "sticking with it," something you just can't do well part-time. Have you ever tried to be a part-time gardener? It just doesn't work—too many weeds!)

One of the hardest jobs on the face of this planet is being a homemaker, and we all should respect anyone who chooses that as an occupation and life's calling. After staying home and taking care of our kids by myself a few times, I was whipped, worn-out, "stick a fork in me" done! It is no job for wimps!! Although this goes against the grain of our modern society, it still strikes a note within women everywhere: to feel comfortable if they desire in their hearts to be homemakers. We need to have a better balance.

When I met my wife, Julie, she was employed as a professional makeup artist for TV. I found her to be very approachable, friendly, attractive…but not stuck on being a "career woman." There were a lot of qualities in her that really drew me to her—qualities that were very different from those of a lot of women I had met in Nashville who were willing to do anything to advance their careers. Julie can sing—but she doesn't want to be a singer. Julie is pretty—but she doesn't want to be a beauty queen. I have learned (from being married to her) that Julie loves to sing with our children, she loves to make our home a beautiful refuge, she is talented and charming…and she loves to be a homemaker. She doesn't try to be somebody

It's plain to see that
she's not seeking

Glory on this Earth.

She believes in honesty,

And the joy of giving birth.

"(She Wants to Be a)
Homemaker"
by Paul Overstreet and Dan
Tyler. Scarlet Moon Music
(BMI) Screen Gems-EMI
Music, Inc. (BMI) A Little
More Music, Inc. (ASCAP)
Sharp Circle Music (ASCAP).
1988.

Awards
"Forever and Ever, Amen"
1988 *Nashville Network*
Viewers Choice Awards

About Paul Overstreet

Launching a Career

(continued)

"When You Say Nothing at All," sung by the British artist Ronan Keating, was part of the soundtrack for the movie, *Notting Hill*. Paul also had a hand in writing "Love Can Build a Bridge," a Grammy winner recorded by the Judds. Other hits have been recorded by Glen Campbell, Pam Tillis, Mel Tillis, Travis Tritt, the Forester Sisters, Marie Osmond, and Michael Martin Murphy.

Most recently, Paul has had two songs recorded by Kenny Chesney on his *Everywhere We Go* CD: "She Thinks My Tractor's Sexy," and the title cut.

(More about Paul Overstreet in Chapter 11)

other than who she is—and that continues to appeal to me.

Here's what Julie herself has to say about this song:

In a nutshell, Paul was able to write a song for all women who are home-makers...but he went much farther than just "validating" them in a time when they and their husbands have to explain their chosen path with an almost apologetic tone—he made people see homemakers as beautiful, desirable, wise, important, talented, joyful, contented, unselfish, and hardworking!

Although some people may never see this, his song made it possible for these "politically incorrect" couples to feel satisfaction and pride in their career choices—some maybe for the first time...others perhaps for the first time in a long time where they were affirmed in their choice—and in the world we live in, that's controversial!

I also like that Paul used the term "homemaker" rather than "stay-at-home Mom." I believe you can be a homemaker before you ever have children and long after they are gone—it is a mind-set and a belief system. Those who really hear this song say, "Thanks for saying it, and thanks for living it." That's what Paul's song is about.

Letters

⇌ A Glow That Has Never Faded ⇌

*A*s a high school student, my daughter, Glynnis, knew that God had equipped her with everything she needed to be successful at what He had called her to do. Although I work in a professional atmosphere, it took me a long time to finally accept that she would not be going to college. Anytime my colleagues learned that my daughter planned to work to help send her boyfriend to college because she wanted to be a housewife, they would immediately attack her for all the reasons drawn from today's definition of success. She always felt inferior for following what God put in her. She would hedge her answers, saying she was going to work for awhile before going to school. This caused real self-esteem problems.

One night, her boyfriend drove her around town playing and singing "Homemaker" from Paul Overstreet's tape. She came home in tears, with such a glow that has never faded. I am pleased to say that Glynnis and Moses have been married five and a half years, and have two of the most beautiful children you have ever seen. Glynnis gets to stay home with those children and make a home for Moses, who loves to be in that home. They are applying God's Word to their relationship with each other and with their children.

"My daughter used that song as a stepping-stone into being what God has called her to be, and not trying to adhere to the standards of the world. She is wise beyond her years."

**"(She Wants to Be a)
Homemaker"**
was included on the album,
Sowin' Love released in
1989, along with these
additional songs:

Love Helps Those Who
Cannot Help Themselves

All the Fun

Call the Preacher

Richest Man on Earth

Sowin' Love

Love Never Sleeps

Dig Another Well

Seein' My Father in Me

What God Has Joined
Together

'Neath the Light
of Your Love

(BMG Music; RCA Corporation)

My daughter used that song as a stepping-stone into being what God has called her to be, and not trying to adhere to the standards of the world. She is wise beyond her years. I keep a copy of that CD in my car and play it all the time. I was being stared at and wondered why—my friend told me it was because we were a car full of blacks and Mexicans playing Country music loudly! Thank God for Paul Overstreet!

—**Diane S.; Lancaster, Texas**

❧ Singing This Song All the Time ❧

My father is a Baptist minister; so, like Paul, I grew up in the limelight of the church. Proverbs 31 has always been my aspiration. I fell out of God's will—as so many of us have at some time in our lives—but I always had the strength, through Him, to go on. After an unplanned, unwed pregnancy, I found the man of my dreams. He is short, heavy and balding, and 12 years my senior!

All I wanted was to be a "Homemaker," and although I am a mother of three (I count my daughter, who was adopted out through Jerry Falwell's Home for Unwed Mothers), I find that I still feel as though being a homemaker is the most prestigious job I could hold. I went on to become a pediatric nurse. I find myself singing that song all the time. My face will not grace TV screens, and I may sing off-key, but my children think I'm beautiful and that I can "fix anything" because, after all, "You're a 'peteractive' nurse, Mommy!"

Mr. Overstreet, of all the church songs and Country songs and any other songs, I don't

know of any other person who could have captured what God has intended for our lives as
women. I am a nurse, and have prestige and
confidence in what I do, but I live for Christ
and I strive to be a good "Homemaker."

—**Linda A.**

❧ New Dreams ❧

I had a tough childhood. A single mother
with five kids to raise doesn't have a whole
lot of time to spend with her kids. I pretty
much had to raise myself since my siblings
were all so much older than me. Needless to
say, I was starved for attention and affection.

When I was 13, we moved to Oklahoma City,
and suddenly I was the popular girl in school.
Never being faced with peer pressure before, I
was sucked into a few things that I am not proud
of. I found out shortly after my 14th birthday
that I was pregnant. I did a good job of hiding
it for seven months, terrified of disappointing my

> "I sing [my wife-
> to-be] this lovely
> song, and it
> brings tears to
> my eyes—you
> know what love
> is and what a
> homemaker
> truly is."

"Diamonds in the rough"—Chord and Nash

"...for all of the husbands who maybe don't know just how to say it—Paul's song says it all. Love is the key to being happy, and with time, comes great wisdom."

mother; but sooner or later, she had to find out. But she was terrific, and a couple of months later, we had a tiny new addition to the family.

At the time, my mother was working at a radio station in Oklahoma City, and she was always bringing home promo cassettes that she got from the station. One of those cassettes was yours. A brand-new mom, a total outcast with all my friends (who were terrified that their parents might find out they were friends with such a loser), there wasn't much more to do with my spare time besides drown myself in music. There was one particular song that held special meaning to me. When I found out I was pregnant, I knew that all the plans I had made for my future would be unrealistic now, so I made up my mind that I would concentrate all my efforts on making my little family as happy as I possibly could.

For several years, I played "Homemaker" every day. Every single morning, I would play it over and over, as loudly as I could. It made me realize that, yes, I have made mistakes and my dreams had come to an end, but my life did not have to—I could just come up with new dreams.

—**Merilee V.; Russellville, Arkansas**

❧ Described to a "T" ❧

Paul's song, "Homemaker" has described me to a "T" for years. I had a painful event happen to me, and God gave me a song to help me get through it. I thought my dream was an impossibility and was willing to accept the life of a single mother as the one God planned for *me. Recently I met a man who has shown me that my dream of being a homemaker with a real family doesn't have to change. Every time I play Paul's song, I can see my fiancé's face, and I am the one thanking God for His graciousness. Thank Paul for his inspiration in my life.*

—**Cheryl M.; Lombard, Illinois, USA**

∾ Many Blessings ∾

I fell in love with Paul Overstreet's music the first time I heard his "Sowin' Love" album. Every song reminded me of my parents, and I honestly don't think I have ever been so touched by any piece of music. I particularly like the songs "Homemaker" and "All the Fun," because that just encompasses my mom and dad's lives—it's as if he was singing every song on that album just for us. I'm proud to say that my mother is a homemaker, and Dad would far rather come home to my mom's love than stay out with his welding buddies.

Now, after seven years of loving Paul Overstreet's music, the words hold much deeper meaning for me. I am married to the most kind and gentle man I've ever had the pleasure of meeting. We have two little girls. I am blessed with the opportunity to follow in my mother's footsteps and be a homemaker myself. I cry when I hear that song, and think it has words that any wife would love to hear from her husband. At the same time, for all of the husbands who maybe don't know just how to say it—Paul's song says it all. Love is the key to being happy, and with time, comes great wisdom.

"With the love of a great family and faith in a higher power, comes everything your heart desires."

> *"Everyone should have the chance to have some-thing this meaningful and beautiful enter into their soul. Thank you, Paul, for filling my home with such beautiful music."*

With the love of a great family and faith in a higher power, comes everything your heart desires. With that, you gain the strength to persevere over any obstacle, and come out a better person afterward.

The music of Paul Overstreet is a blessing to myself and my family. I feel uplifted every time it's played. If more people felt this way, the world would be a much nicer place. Everyone should have the chance to have something this meaningful and beautiful enter into their soul. Thank you, Paul, for filling my home with such beautiful music...you are a very special man.

—**Aimee G.; Marshall,
Saskatchewan, Canada**

❧ Exactly His Fiancée ❧

Your song, "Homemaker," is exactly what my wife-to-be, Deborah Lynne, is all about. The song dovetails into every aspect of her life and what she truly is. I sing her this lovely song, and it brings tears to my eyes—you know what love is and what a homemaker truly is. I bought this album, and I have kept it with me...until the day I met her, and found that she is everything you wrote and sang about. Thank you, Mr. Overstreet, for touching our lives in a way that I can never forget.

—**Surendran S.**

Chapter 11

Heroes

Personally, this song challenged me for a long, long time. First of all, I don't usually put music to lyrics that someone wrote; secondly, I don't accept lyrics through the mail. I said all that to say: this was an unusual process for me! It began one day at *Capitol Records,* when I was introduced to this lady, Claire Cloninger. She had been there for a meeting with a friend of mine; she was leaving as I was going in. She had the sweetest, quiet spirit about her. I was told that she wrote a lot of songs in the Christian music field. We also had another mutual friend, a really good singer whom I had worked with from time to time, Kelly Willard. Kelly talked a lot about Claire.

I don't remember the exact timetable, but at some point, I received some lyrics from Claire. I didn't really know what to do

Verse One

He drives into the city,

Works extra hard all day;

Finishes up early,

So he can get away.

'Cause there's a blue-eyed kid on second base,

Wants Dad to watch him play.

Daddy knows he's waiting,

So he hurries on his way.

Chorus

'Cause you know heroes
come in every shape
and size,

Making special sacrifices
for others in their lives.

No one gives them medals,

The world don't
know their names;

But in someone's eyes,

They're heroes
just the same.

Verse Two

She rocks her crying baby

In the hour before dawn;

She whispers
words of hope

To help her
husband to hold on.

She takes time
for the children,

Making sure they
know she cares;

She's more than a Mama,

She's the answer
to their prayers.

with them because I don't usually put music to already-written lyrics. So I just stuck them on my dresser by the door of our bedroom. They must have laid there for weeks. I started to put them away several times. Each time, there was a line in the first verse that kept grabbing me: *"a blue-eyed boy on second base wants Dad to watch him play."* Every time I would read that, I'd get this lump in my throat.

I couldn't figure out what it was about that particular line that was doing that to me! Was it the fact that my dad and mom had divorced when I was young… and Dad had moved to California, and was not around to see me play ball? Or was it that I knew it would be so great if I didn't miss that important father-son relationship aspect with my own sons? I don't know—maybe it was a little of both.

Anyway, those lyrics kept getting my attention. So I finally called Claire, and we found some time to get together and work on the song. After we wrote it and made a work-tape of it, it sat in my studio for a long time on this ledge by my console. As I began looking for songs for the *Heroes* album, I had not put that song in the batch…but it kept staring at me from that ledge every day and I looked at it every day.

We were down to the last meetings before going into the studio and recording, and the president of *RCA Records* said, "You know, we're still missing that one song—

Heroes — page 85

that kind of "Seein' My Father in Me" kind of song. We need a song like that for this album." So I started looking around, and found some songs that I thought might do it. I was headed in for the meeting to play him the songs…and on my way out of the studio, I saw that tape on the ledge. I picked it up, put it in my pocket, and went to the meeting. After we listened to all the songs I had brought, I pulled it out. When he heard the first verse and chorus, he said, "That's it! That's the one!"

When I think of how close I come to missing God…sometimes I'm so thankful He stays after me. And, by the way, I *have* a blue-eyed boy who loves baseball…and he will *never* want me to watch him play as much as I love watching him play!

Letters

His Way of Saying "Thanks, Mom"

When I was 18, I was forced to move out of my parents' house by my stepfather. This happened without my mother's knowledge. By the time that she found out about the "arrangement," I had already moved most of my things and I had decided that I couldn't live with him anymore, so I went through with the move. My mother and I have always been very close. She had me at the age of 15, and very

Bridge

Now I don't pretend to know you,

But I bet it's safe to say,

There's someone out there somewhere

Looking up to you today.

And they see everything you do,

Except for your mistakes;

You may not think you measure up,

But you've got all it takes.

Tag

Yeah, in someone else's eyes,

They're heroes just the same.

Talking about heroes, special kind of heroes,

No ordinary heroes …

"Heroes" by Paul Overstreet and Claire Cloninger. Scarlet Moon Music (BMI) ~ Juniper Landing Music (ASCAP). 1990.

About Paul Overstreet

Producing Music

In addition to being a writer and an artist, Paul is also an accomplished producer. He co-produces his own albums, his most recent being *A Songwriter's Project, Volume One*, and his Christian CD, *Living by The Book*, and was sole producer for Christian Country artist Suzie Luchsinger (the album that launched her career). Paul also co-wrote many songs for that project, two of which topped the Christian Country charts (one was a duet they performed together).

(More about Paul Overstreet in Chapter 12)

———⊳•0•⊲———

soon thereafter we were in Germany. My father was in the Army and always out in the field, so my mother and I sort of grew up together.

Well, while I was moving the rest of my things, my mother was crying and saying that she had failed me as a mother. I had only one Paul Overstreet tape at the time. I put it in my Walkman and set it up to start at the song titled, "Heroes." I asked my mother to listen to a song for me, because I wanted her opinion. I pushed "play," set it down and finished packing and moving my things.

About ten minutes later, I hadn't heard anything from her, so I went into the living room, where she sat crying even harder than before. I knew the song had the desired effect on her. Having grown up mentally and emotionally a lot sooner than most people my age, and seeing a young mother struggle and sacrifice everything for her children, to me that song says everything I've ever felt towards my mother. It was a way for me to say, "Thank you, Mom, for everything." Being a father myself now, I hope one day my son—under different circumstances—will ask me to listen to a song called "Seein' My Father in Me." Thank you, Mr. Overstreet.

—**Christopher N.**

❧ Music Touched Everything She Did ❧

I have been a fan of Paul's for many years. My mom was ill with cancer, and the only thing that seemed to help me get through it was Paul's music. My favorite song, which made me think of my mom, is "Heroes." I would care for Mom and listen to Paul in my headphones.

She passed away March 1996. I saw Paul that June at a Franklin Graham crusade. I live in New Hampshire, and I never thought I'd get to see him live unless I went down south. I told Paul about this, but it wasn't until later that I heard his sister had passed away from cancer around the same time as my mom. His music touches everything I do!

—Marie D.; Belmont, New Hampshire

Saw Christ in Many of the Songs

My heart was at a spiritual junction just as "Heroes" came out. My little boy thought the world began and ended with me. I saw him in the song, and my wife also. I couldn't always bear to hear it, but I loved it. The whole album has deep meaning for me, especially "Center of My Storm," the first Overstreet song I sang before my church. I saw Christ in so many of the songs. God used "Heroes" to soften my heart and seal a relationship with Jesus Christ. Thanks, Paul.

—Walt A.; Jackson, New Jersey

Songwriter's Inspiration

Early in 1991, I drove to Nashville to play Writers Night at the Bluebird Café. While I was there, I was able to sing and play for a

"I have been a fan of Paul's for many years. My mom was ill with cancer, and the only thing that seemed to help me get through it was Paul's music. My favorite song, which made me think of my mom, is 'Heroes.'"

"God used 'Heroes' to soften my heart and seal a relationship with Jesus Christ."

record producer. He said I had what it takes to be a performer, but he didn't hear any "hooks" in my songs. He suggested I study the songwriting talents of a guy named Paul Overstreet. He told me to listen to Paul's album, "Heroes." Well, I picked up the "Heroes" tape and left Nashville for Newark, Delaware, my home town. I drove in a terrible rainstorm. I was unfamiliar with the mountain road and visibility was poor, so I followed the taillights of the 18-wheelers until I was out of the storm. All that time, I listened to Paul's "Heroes" album and was simply amazed at his writing talent.

I went home and wrote song after song...Eventually I went back to writing Soft Rock, because that's who I am. But studying Paul Overstreet's talent for songwriting has made me a finer writer...I can say that my songs all have the "hooks" now and more. Even though I had never heard of Paul Overstreet in my life, I will never forget him.

—**Joe C.; Newark, Delaware**

Paul with Franklin Graham at a Samaritan's Purse event

❧ Inspired to Be a "Hero" ❧

Your song, "Heroes," has a special meaning to me. All my life I always wished someone would make me feel so important to them. Unfortunately it never happened, but one thing I could do for myself was to try and make others feel important in life. So whenever someone I knew or worked with was going through a crisis, had something happy to celebrate, or just needed a lift, I would write a few lines of poetry, and it would always seem to make their day. It was through your song, "Heroes," that brought what was missing in my life and gave me the insight to be a hero in someone else's life.

—Diana S.; Valrico, Florida, USA

❧ Father Turned "Hero" ❧

Did you know that one of your fans lives in a village in the Swiss mountains? Unfortunately, I missed your concert in Frutigen in 1989, but I heard it on the radio. Your song, "Heroes," was a great encouragement to me in 1992; after the birth of our third child, my wife felt very weak for a long time, and so I had to care for the family, and there was still my professional working. I didn't feel like a "hero"—I felt tired and sometimes sad. But your song, "Heroes" (and other songs about the family) helped me carry on through that situation. Thank you very much for your wonderful music! Congratulations on your sixth child! God bless you and your family.

—Martin Z.; Igis,
Graubuenden, Switzerland

"Heroes"
was included on the album,
Heroes *released in 1990,*
along with these
additional songs:

Ball and Chain

If I Could Bottle This Up

Daddy's Come Around

Love Lives On

I'm So Glad I Was Dreaming

Straight and Narrow

Billy Can't Read

She Supports Her Man

'Til the Mountains
Disappear

The Calm at the
Center of My Storm

(BMG Music; RCA Corporation)

"I didn't feel like a 'hero'— I felt tired and sometimes sad. But your song, 'Heroes' (and other songs about the family) helped me carry on through that situation."

❧ Blessed by the Music ❧

Your songs brought tears to my eyes. I listened to you in my worldly days of "honky tonking," and longed for the things you sang about. I can remember listening to your "Heroes" CD over and over, writing pages of hopeless poetry. Now I am saved, married, and have three children [ages] four and under. The Lord has blessed me richly. And your music has blessed me as well.

—**Monica C.; O'Fallon, Missouri**

❧ A Turning Point ❧

About eight years ago, I found myself single and pregnant. The father of my child was not willing to help in any way to support me or my baby emotionally or financially. I was devastated and did not feel that I would be able to go through with my pregnancy, much less to raise a child on my own. I had contacted some abortion clinics to find out about costs and procedures, but I felt very guilty because I knew that was not the right thing to do. I prayed that God would send me some sort of sign so that I would know what to do.

I worked for a Country radio station, and we were promoting a concert for Paul Overstreet. He would be performing at Abilene Christian University. In my emotional state, I did not feel like attending, but some of my friends and co-workers encouraged me to go. That night would prove to be a turning point in my life.

Paul came onstage and sang a few songs. He then announced a very special dedication. He recognized a group of pregnant single mothers who were at the concert that night. He spoke of their courage and dedicated the song "Heroes" to them. At that moment, I knew that God was giving me the answer that I had asked for. I listened to every word in the song, and it brought me to tears. I suddenly knew what I needed to do!

Now I am proud to say that I am Mommy to a beautiful seven-year old girl named Kendyl, who makes straight A's in her second grade class. She is also a little beauty queen, and has won twenty trophies and two crowns in the last two years. She is so sweet and very special, and she changed my life for the better! Whenever I hear the song, "Heroes," I always remember that night, and how it helped to change the course of my life!

—Kelly A.; Abilene, Texas, USA

❧ Heroes Behind Greatness ❧

I felt always that behind every great man or woman there are a lot of heroes, unknown people who gave their life and time for love and for nothing else. Everywhere in the world you'll find this kind of people: doctors, teachers, DJs, home workers, etc.; volunteers against any kind of discrimination and all the bad things of this world. Nobody will know their name, but in someone's heart they are the "Heroes" of life. Without them, the world would be absolute a misery. I love this song, and I always have loved this people. They mean a lot to me.

—Rafel C.; Palafrugell,
Costa Brava, Spain

> *"He recognized a group of pregnant single mothers who were at the concert that night. He spoke of their courage and dedicated the song 'Heroes' to them. At that moment, I knew that God was giving me the answer that I had asked for."*

———⋙◦⋘———

"...he wrote about a wife supporting her husband faithfully and how she was a hero. I began to cry and looked at [my wife], and we squeezed hands. It was a moment I shall always remember..."

———⋙◦⋘———

≈ A Moment to Always Remember ≈

I first heard Paul's music while visiting with my wife in Gatlinburg, Tennessee. We were in a Christian bookstore and his tape was playing over the sound system, and I was taken with the depth of the music's message and yet the simplicity of it. I immediately knew that I was listening to someone who shared my values concerning making family a priority. I bought the tape only hearing the one song, and then gradually bought the others as they were produced.

So many of his songs have benefited our family, but one very special moment stands out among the others. I am a pastor, and was going through some deep valleys in our ministry, especially financially. My wife has always stood by me, and never suggested that I seek anything else to do although it meant sacrifice for us sometimes. On the way home, with the children in the back seat and my dear wife beside me, the song "Heroes" was playing...and I was soaking up every line. I sure didn't feel like much of a hero at all, but a first-class failure. In the second verse, he wrote about a wife supporting her husband faithfully and how she was a hero. I began to cry and looked at her, and we squeezed hands. It was a moment I shall always remember, and it strengthened me and allowed me to thank God for the faithful support of a godly wife. Thanks, Paul, for allowing God to use you. I hope to be able to meet you some day.

—Rick J.; Huntsville, Alabama

Chapter 12

Daddy's Come Around (to Mama's Way of Thinking)

One day, one of my co-writers, Don Schlitz, told me about how he and his wife, Polly, were vigorously discussing the issue of whether or not he should do something one way when she said he should do it the other way. He said, "As the day went on, I realized that I was now doing things just the way Polly had said to do it…" (he never told me exactly what it was) "…and it dawned on me, 'Well, it looks like Daddy has come around to Mama's way of thinking.'" Then he added something like, "You may not like it, but I just thought I'd mention it as an idea to work on."

I was thinking, "Are you nuts? I love it!"—and we went right to work. We wrote that song that day, and we had a lot of fun with it. After we made a "demonstration recording" of the song, it got pitched

Chorus

Daddy's come around to
Mama's way of thinking;

No more staying out
all night drinking.

Everything's better
on the home front now;

They're meeting
in the middle,

And they're working it out.

He's finally figured
he's got something
worth keeping;

(Yeah, my) Daddy's
come around to
Mama's way of thinking.

Verse One

Daddy used to go
out every night
with his friends;

Mama stayed home
taking care of the kids.

Daddy didn't mind
the way it was arranged;

To his way of thinking,
it didn't seem strange.

Then one night, Mama
met Daddy at the door,

'Cause the key in his hand
didn't work anymore.

Mama said, "More than
the locks have changed;

There's a new set of
rules to this old game."

Verse Two

It's been some time since
she laid down the law,

But Daddy don't seem
to mind at all.

He comes straight home
when the work-day's
through;

He's even done the dishes
a time or two.

around town, and a new group picked it up and put it on hold. That's meant—in the Nashville songwriting business—that they were planning on recording it the next time they made a record. I secretly wanted to record it myself; but as a writer and a recording artist too, I always tried to be considerate of my co-writers and never tie up songs that we could get recorded by another artist.

Well, as things sometimes happen, I was beginning a new record for *RCA* when I got the news that the group who had that song on hold no longer wanted to record it. Wow, I jumped on it! This song became the fastest-moving chart record I had, and made it all the way to the number one spot in the nation. Not only was it a fun record...but it was doing a lot of good out there that I had not even thought about.

A woman once wrote to let me know that she didn't know me or had ever heard of my music before, until recently. Her husband had moved out, leaving her and her two boys. He had moved in with another woman. Then one day—out of the blue—she got a call from him, asking if she would agree to meet with him for lunch. She apprehensively said she would. While at lunch, he said he wanted to play a song for her. She thought, *This is a little strange.* He then played a recording of "Daddy's Come Around" for her—which was a little more strange, because she didn't listen to Country music! After the song finished playing, he told her he had been doing a lot of thinking, and wanted to know if she would consider giving him another chance. She wrote me to let me know that she did give him another chance. Now she had her husband back...but most of all, her boys now have their daddy back! Hey, isn't that what happens when you play a Country song backwards?

There was a young man in Portland, Oregon who told me a story about how "Daddy's Come Around..." had changed his life. We were playing at an annual outdoor festival held on the banks of the river. Long before our show, this young man made his way back to the trailers where the performers were waiting. He somehow got past the security and located me. He began by telling me he was parked down by this same river one night. He was sitting in his car with a loaded pistol and a six-pack of beer; he later told me he was also a heroin addict. On this particular night, he was going to end it all. He had already written a goodbye note to his wife, who was a Christian, and their kids. He was going to kill himself. His radio was tuned to a Country station, and they played the new single we had just released on *RCA Records*: "Daddy's Come Around." He said that the song stopped him right there. He threw the beer and the gun into the river, and went back home to his wife and kids. The next day, he checked himself into a drug rehab center.

I am totally astonished that someone would hear a song like "Daddy's Come Around" and it could have that kind of effect

Late last night, when the lights were low,

Daddy told Mama, "I love you so."

Early this morning, Mama said to him,

"You just might get to be a Daddy again."

"Daddy's Come Around" by Paul Overstreet and Don Schlitz. Scarlet Moon Music (BMI) ~ Don Schlitz Music; All Rights Administered by Almo Music Corp. (ASCAP) for the World. 1990.

Awards
"Love Is Strong" 1992 *Dove Award* (Gospel Music Association) Country Recorded Album of the Year

About Paul Overstreet

Music and Family

Paul Overstreet is known for songs that encourage the family, and has lived that out in his own life, turning down many "opportunities" to be on the road—for "opportunities" to stay close to home as his children grow up. Having his own recording studio on his farm (west of Nashville) has made that part a little easier. He has just released *A Songwriter's Project, Volume One* as a songwriter, artist and producer. This has been a labor of love, one much awaited by those who will love Paul's own rendering of his hit songs previously recorded by other artists. There are also a couple of his own brand-new cuts included on this new CD. The CD was released by

on them! That's not what I think about when we sit in some tiny room and pound out a lyric. I never, ever conceived that a song would touch someone in that way...not until I started hearing these stories!

This goes far and beyond what our mortal minds can fathom. That is why I believe that God takes our mere efforts and transforms them into something He uses in others' lives to encourage, admonish, lift up—whatever He desires. It is because of this phenomenon that I believe we writers have a tremendous responsibility...we should consider all our options and ask ourselves, "What will I do with the three-and-a-half minutes (the time it takes to listen to an average radio song) of someone's time? What will I give them? Will it be hope, a challenge, or comfort in doing something they know is right and good?"

I don't think for a minute that this story—or any of the others—should bring glory to me or the other writers with whom the songs were written. We have our good days and our bad. But rather, the glory should be given to God for allowing us, in some small way, to be a part of what He has done for someone else. This song wasn't really very well accepted when we first took it to the record companies, but it went on to become a number one hit...because it just tells the truth, just the way it is. I'm glad that my songs don't cause people to go out and get divorced, or cause a 16-year old girl to go out and get pregnant.

Letters

➣ A Song With Victory ➣

"**D**addy's Come Around" has always been very special to me. I truly believe that, with the Lord's help, anyone can turn their life and marriage around for the better. My husband chose not to seek the Lord for his alcohol addiction, and we were divorced in December 1998. I still love him, and the story is not over as long as my ex-husband has breath. He can still surrender his life to the only One who can heal him. Thanks, Paul, for a wonderful song with victory in it. Not all marriages have to end in divorce, right?

—**Joanne M.; Hanover, Ontario, Canada**

Scarlet Moon Records as "Volume One" (always leave them wanting more!), and with Paul's God-given talent, that's not hard to do. Also just released is his latest Christian CD, *Living by the Book,* a wonderful new collection of 13 offerings.

(More about Paul Overstreet in Chapter 13)

Now we know why Paul wears his cowboy hat. Paul and Charity.

"It was during this dark time that a flicker of light and hope appeared. That ray of light was in the music and lyrics of your music… you painted a picture for me of what a Christian family could look like."

❧ Spiritual Awakening ❧

*T*his letter is long overdue. For years I have wanted you to know how much you and your music have meant to me. It was eight years ago that I was coming to the end of myself—as a man, husband, and father. A married man with a six-year old son and a two-year old daughter, I was struggling with depression and hopelessness after years of alcohol and drug abuse. I didn't understand why—even after putting the liquor behind me, and with a beautiful wife and family—I could be in so much pain. I was numb. Fear, confusion and a deep feeling of inadequacy overwhelmed me.

It was during this dark time that a flicker of light and hope appeared. That ray of light was in the music and lyrics of your music…you painted a picture for me of what a Christian family could look like. I knew that picture was not my family and that loving "Daddy" was not me—but oh, did you put a desire in my heart to make that picture a reality in my life! Between your songs, and watching my wife in her growing relationship with Christ, I felt drawn to this loving God. The kind of life you sang about—and, no doubt, lived—was very appealing to me and put into my heart a desire to seek God for His forgiveness and healing. I would weep at my failings and inadequacies as a father, and pray that God would put enough love into my heart to love my family the way the daddy in your songs did. As I was a singer in a wedding band—and, at that time, also a

Country singer—your music was a fitting "instrument" in God's hands to get through to me right where I was.

Mr. Overstreet, the Lord used your music and talent as a spiritual awakening which led to my salvation. Praise the Lord! It's been eight years now, and my wife of seventeen years, our fourteen-year old son and ten-year old daughter, all have the husband, daddy and home life they never would have experienced had it not been for the grace of God. I've thanked God for your ministry for all these years, and will continue to pray for you.

—Rick S.; San Francisco, California

"Daddy's Come Around" was included on the album, **Heroes** released in 1990, along with these additional songs:

Ball and Chain

If I Could Bottle This Up

Love Lives On

Heroes

I'm So Glad I Was Dreaming

Straight and Narrow

Billy Can't Read

She Supports Her Man

'Til the Mountains Disappear

The Calm at the Center of My Storm

(BMG Music; RCA Corporation)

Paul communicates with his audience.

Chapter 13

When You Say Nothing at All

Perhaps the real story behind this song is the history of all the different artists who have recorded it. Don Schlitz and I wrote it; it was played for Keith Whitley and his producer, Garth Fundis; they liked it and recorded it. Keith was just a young guy, early thirties, who was one of the best Country singers we had in our industry. He came up through Bluegrass music about the same time as Ricky Skaggs.

Keith got caught up in the world of alcohol and other things that are so prevalent in our business. I spent a small amount of time with Keith and his wife, Lori Morgan, on a ski trip we took to Colorado. He really seemed to be doing great at that time. He had stopped drinking and had a good thing going with Lori. He seemed at peace.

It was sometime after that Colorado trip that he recorded and released the

Verse One

It's amazing how you can
speak right to my heart;

Without saying a word,
you can light up the dark.

Try as I may,
I could never explain

What I hear when you
don't say a thing.

Chorus

The smile on your face

Lets me know
that you need me.

There's a truth
in your eyes

Saying you'll
never leave me.

A touch of your
hands says

You'll catch me
if I ever fall.

Yeah, you can say it best

When you say
nothing at all.

Verse Two

All day long, I can hear
people talking out loud;

But when you hold me
near, you drown
out the crowd.

Old Mister Webster
could never define

What's being said between
your heart and mine.

"When You Say Nothing at
All" by Paul Overstreet and
Don Schlitz. Scarlet Moon
Music (BMI) Writers Group
Music (BMI) MCA Music
(a Division of MCA, Inc.)
(ASCAP) Don Schlitz Music
(ASCAP). 1988.

song, "When You Say Nothing at All." Keith had actually recorded several of our songs, including "On the Other Hand"—the song with which Randy Travis has such a big record. He recorded another song I had written with Dan Tyler and Fred Knobloch called "Somebody's Doin' Me Right," which was released after his death.

I was so shocked when I heard that Keith had died of an alcohol and drug overdose. I thought he was on the right road, and had that part of his life straightened out...but I guess we just never know what someone is dealing with.

Years after his death, his wife, Lori, along with *RCA Records,* began putting together a tribute album for Keith, and Alison Krause chose to sing "When You Say Nothing at All" on it. I have always thought she has a voice like an angel. When I heard her recording, the hair on my arms and the back of my neck stood straight up—it was incredible. I didn't know what would happen with it, but I knew it was a great rendition of the song. It hadn't been that long since Keith had a big record on that song, so I didn't know if it would be a single or not...but the song was a favorite once again, and was heard around the world on Country stations and all kinds of stations because of Alison's great performance.

When I met Alison, she told me an incredible story about a lady whose daughter had a disability, and how this song had affected their relationship. When we were reading the stories submitted for this book, I was so pleasantly surprised to find that story had been submitted; you'll read it below ("Indirect Tribute").

Once I was doing some work on our farm, and I had just bought a John Deere tractor with a cab. It's tough on a singer to do any bush-hogging with all the dust and pollen flying around, so I told myself that I really needed that tractor; I was a little concerned about the price, but I kept convincing myself it was practical. This tractor has a radio in the cab. One day, I was riding around the field, listening to a Light Rock station, and I heard an introduction to a song come on. I thought, "That sounds familiar"—and it was "When You Say Nothing at All." At that moment, I felt a little better about buying the tractor.

Somewhere in the scheme of things, a guy who was a movie producer in the United Kingdom heard the song performed by Alison, and decided he wanted to use it at some point in one of his movies. When he began working on the movie called *Notting Hill* (starring Julia Roberts and Hugh Grant), he thought that this would be a good movie for that song. He had a young Pop artist named Ronan Keating sing it for the soundtrack.

The production was great, and I loved that version also. It was the first time I had experienced a Pop act recording one of

About Paul Overstreet

Paul's Heart for Missions

Paul also gives much of his time to helping others. "One of the joys of my life has been working with my friend, Franklin Graham, the president of Samaritan's Purse. This ministry is an international relief organization committed to meeting the spiritual and physical needs of people in crisis situations.

(More about Paul Overstreet in Chapter 14)

"When You Say Nothing at All" was included on the album, **A Songwriter's Project– Volume One** *released in August, 2000, along with these additional songs:*

Same Ole Me

I Won't Take Less Than Your Love

When You Say Nothing at All

Forever and Ever, Amen

A Long Line of Love

Diggin' Up Bones

Be Mine

On the Other Hand

I Fell in Love Again Last Night

Toughest Battles

What Are Friends For

When Mama Ain't Happy

(BMG Music; RCA Corporation)

our songs. We got together with several of our friends, and went to see the movie to hear one of our songs being used. What a feeling that was—sitting there in the theater, hearing the song that I had been fortunate enough to be a part of, surrounded by all the video footage. The song had found its own way, with its simple little message of love, onto the silver screen.

This recording of the song was eventually released as a single with the Irish Group, Boy Zone, as a Pop record in the United Kingdom and most of the rest of the world. It did really well. I would love to see them release it here in the United States as a Pop record one day. I like the way this song expresses how people—especially when they're in love—can communicate without ever saying a word. I guess love really does have its own language.

Letters

❦ **Their Perfect Song** ❦

I live in a small town in Oregon where the music scene is non-existent. My boyfriend talked me into Karaoke one night; he knew I liked to sing. Your song, "When You Say Nothing at All," was special for us already, and it was the only one I could think of. It was perfect, like it was written for me to sing to him. We became regulars for awhile, and that song became mine for him. It got us through a lot of hard nights. Unfortunately, a very tragic accident event took him from me. I still sing that song for him. Thank you for writing such a perfect song, and for giving us that perfect moment.

—**Susan R.; North Bend, Oregon**

≈ Tears of Joy ≈

O*ne of my closest friends asked me to sing at her wedding. She told me her soon-to-be husband wanted "When You Say Nothing at All" sung, and I gladly agreed. As time came closer to the wedding day, my girlfriend and I got very serious about staying together forever. Yeah! So, on the day of my best friend's wedding, I sang not only to my best friend standing at the altar with her new husband...but I sang the song to my soon-to-be wife. Of course, tears of joy filled all of our eyes. Thank you, Paul, for a GREAT song, one of many!*

—**Chris T.**

≈ Life-Changing Song ≈

T*he song, "When You Say Nothing at All," has had a major impact on my life for a few reasons. My favorite musical artist is Alison Krause, and I had been listening to her music for about a year before this single came out. At the time, I was in high school, learning American Sign Language, which eventually*

> *"...that song became mine for him. It got us through a lot of hard nights."*

Everyone gets involved with home-schooling

> *"...when I say that 'When You Say Nothing at All' has impacted my life—it has not only entertained me with its beautiful musical arrangement and lyrics, but it has also brought me to a different level in life."*

would have a huge impact on my life as well. Part of learning ASL entailed learning to sign to songs. This was the first Alison Krause song I learned. I performed it for school talent shows, even at two weddings, before I was able to personally show it to Alison.

Since then, I have signed it onstage with her and the band several times at a few venues in the South and Midwest. I get such a wonderful response from the audiences, whether it is Alison's audience, or my own family and friends. I have since gone on to learn several other songs of Alison's, and even appeared in her video for the song from The Prince of Egypt called, "I Give You to His Heart." So when I say that "When You Say Nothing at All" has impacted my life—it has not only entertained me with its beautiful musical arrangement and lyrics, but it has also brought me to a different level in life. A point where I am more confident in my ability to sign and affect people the same way your song has affected me.

—**Cortney E.; Tampa, Florida**

≈ True Intimacy ≈

I recently viewed a movie titled Notting Hill, in which I heard the song, "When You Say Nothing at All." I absolutely love that song, because it does represent the true intimacy and "oneness" of two people in love, who don't even have to speak to know what the other thinks or feels. I had that kind of relationship one time in my life. This song spoke to my *heart and reminded me of how important it is to reach that level of "knowing" someone. I played the song over and over in that movie to try and figure out who was singing it...but I stumbled on it when I checked out "Family Life Today." You never know when or how God will bless your day—He chose to bless mine today!*

—**Carol R.; Deltona, Florida, USA**

❧ Indirect Tribute ❧

(This is, indirectly, a tribute to
Paul Overstreet's music, through the
music of Alison Krause.)

My 11-year old daughter, Alison, has become an enormous fan of Alison Krause (AK); her devotion to AK's music has impacted Alison's life in delightful and surprising ways. Alison was diagnosed with a rare and devastating form of seizures as an infant called infantile spasms. As a result of infantile spasms, Alison has cerebral palsy, is non-verbal (she can say "Mama," but communicates with informal gestures), and has significant delays in her cognitive and physical development. Alison's cognitive awareness and communication gestures have increased dramatically since listening to AK...Alison has learned to "dance" by rocking back and forth and from side to side. She takes our hands in hers so that we can dance with her...These may seem small to many, but they are major things for Alison to be doing, and it also shows us some of the things she understands.

"... it does represent the true intimacy and 'oneness' of two people in love, who don't even have to speak to know what the other thinks or feels."

Awards

"Love Can Build a Bridge"
1992 *Grammy*
(Songwriter)

AK's music has unlocked a door for Alison, and as a result, her development has flourished far beyond any doctor's expectations for her. She has blossomed like a beautiful butterfly spreading her wings and soaring! We have a much clearer understanding of what and how much Alison understands. I am a true believer that God sends or uses people to help others. God has given AK a tremendous gift, which in turn became a tremendous gift for Alison.

We took Alison to see AK in concert in June 1998, in Jackson, Mississippi. When AK sang Alison's two favorite songs—"Oh, Atlanta" and "When You Say Nothing at All"—Alison was in Heaven!...We believe that AK's music has played a major role in Alison's developmental progress. We will always treasure her and her music.

—**Karen H.**

Paul shares some "tricks of the trade" with Chord.

Chapter 14

Ball and Chain

Everybody used to claim that marriage was like getting a life sentence in prison, locked up with a heavy ball and-chain that was miserable. Guys can really be hard on each other about this "big event" in life. This song is not a slam against my wife or against marriage, but actually just the opposite. Marriage is something to be cherished, not a "cross to bear," so to speak.

When Julie and I planned to get married, we decided to keep it to ourselves—partly because we knew the advice of others would be biased, everyone would be judging us and filtering us through their approval systems; they would not be encouraging. We decided that we wouldn't invite people or have a big wedding—we didn't even tell our families. We just went to our minister's house and said our vows. Years later, our minister, Don Finto, told me, "When I told some people I was doing a wedding that day, I added, 'I sure hope it sticks!'"

Verse One

Back when we made our plans to tie the knot,

My friends, they all laughed at me a lot.

Slapped my back and told me how they thought I was insane;

Said, "Son, you're too young to wear that ball and chain."

Chorus One

(But) love don't feel like a ball and chain to me;

When I'm close to you, my heart feels wild and free.

If you are my jailer,
darling, throw away
the key;

Love don't feel like a ball
and chain to me.

Tag

Love don't feel like a
ball and chain,

It don't feel like a
ball and chain,

Love don't feel like a
ball and chain to me.

Verse Two

I still see my single friends
from time to time,

They ask me how it feels
to walk the line.

Well, I tell them it feels
better than I ever
dreamed it would,

And I would not trade
places with them,
even if I could.

It happened to be Super Bowl Sunday, and after the ceremony, we called Julie's brother—just about at kick-off time—to break the news to him. He was not at all happy about this; I think he was shocked to hear we were married…but also we were interrupting the kick-off of the Super Bowl!

One of the most important things our minister said at our wedding was taken from Ecclesiastes: "Two are better than one, because they have a good reward for their labor. For if they fall, one will lift up his companion…Again, if two lie down together, they will keep warm; but how can one be warm alone?…And *a threefold cord is not quickly broken*" (Eccles. 4:9-12). There have been a lot of times when Julie and I have been stressed…and we have felt something supernatural keeping us together— because the "third cord" in our strand is God! If we didn't have God in our lives and in our marriage, I don't know how we would make it. We have our tough times, our ups and downs, but just like our minister said, that third strand has never broken.

One time at a concert, I brought my wife out on the stage and introduced her to the audience. I told them I was going to dedicate the next song to her—my new single, climbing the charts very fast…but when I said the title, "Ball and Chain"—the audience booed! Then they heard the song, and they soon realized what I was really saying about the joys of marriage…and they loved it.

Letters

➤➤●◄◄

➣ Daniel's Songs ➣

*I*n the spring of 1990, a miracle happened in my life—a beautiful blue-eyed baby boy whom we named Daniel Shawn. He was so incredibly beautiful and so incredibly wanted and dreamed about. We had been married for six years, and had struggled with the pain of infertility for the majority of that time, until this absolute miracle came into our lives. We had just about given up that we would ever hold a newborn and raise a child. Needless to say, our families just went crazy and Daniel had more baby showers than any child around. We lived in the grace of God's love, and our lives were out of some old-time romantic novel.

In 1991, Daniel and I were in the car and heard this song that we both started to "bop" to—it was something about "she wasn't a ball and chain to me." Because Daniel liked it, I went out and bought the CD. After that, we played that CD every day. Daniel and I danced to several songs from that CD. He would hold his arms up to be held after the second or third song, and I would hold him and dance.

On May 12, 1992, I let Daniel, then two, go out in the backyard while I fixed dinner. When I went to call him, he was not in the yard. I yelled and searched. I ran and called 911, and then ran back outside. I went into

Bridge

If it is a crime for a man
to love his wife,

Throw that old book at me,
give me ninety-nine to life.

And I'll spend every
minute, every hour,
every day,

Holding you close,
I don't want to get away.

"Ball and Chain"
by Paul Overstreet and Don
Schlitz. Scarlet Moon Music
(BMI) ~ Don Schlitz Music
(ASCAP). 1990.

➤➤●◄◄

"...'Ball and Chain' came on the radio, and right then I realized why it was that I felt so upset: I still loved him..."

➤➤●◄◄

About Paul Overstreet

Paul's Heart for Missions

(continued)

Paul has traveled with Samaritan's Purse to different countries around the world. This organization rapidly responds to places like Nicaragua, Honduras, and Kosovo by providing services such as food, shelter, clothing, and healthcare in their times of need. What really excites me is that their work is motivated by a compelling desire to share the good news of God's gospel, which is exhibited by Franklin's crusades, as well as the incredible ministry of Samaritan's Purse.

(More about Paul Overstreet in Chapter 15)

the fenced-off area that enclosed our swimming pool, and found our beautiful baby boy in the pool. I pulled him out and screamed for help. The police came running across the yard. Daniel spent three days at Oakland Children's Hospital before my husband and I decided to remove life support. He died in my husband's arms on May 14, surrounded by a large extended family, and plenty of pain and grief.

I used Daniel's songs for his funeral, one song about how love lives on, and the other was about God being the Center of our storm. After Daniel's funeral, so many people commented on how the music touched their hearts, and asked where they could get the music. In September 1992, my husband took me to see Paul Overstreet at the Circle Star Theatre, and I curled up and cried throughout the concert (no offense). After Daniel died, I listened to this CD every day and it gave me peace. You never get over losing a child (a miracle), but you can find a little peace. Thank you for the beautiful music that gave me a certain amount of comfort during a nightmare.

—**Bridgett O.**

"Overstreet as a Second Language"

*P*aul's music has always been a blessing in my life. I can remember a time on Country radio when you could tell—no matter who was singing—that you were hearing another great Paul Overstreet song! My wife is Danish and we live in Denmark with our two-year-old *daughter, Savannah. One day we put on Paul's first* Greatest Hits *CD, and it has become Savannah's favorite—a child for whom English is a second language runs around singing, "Love don't feel like a ball and chain to me." For my wife and I—whenever it all gets too much, when we feel like throwing in the towel—we listen and "Take Another Run" at it. I am not the kind of guy who writes to recording artists, but Paul Overstreet is not just another recording artist. I can't wait to get to the States and get the new CD!*

—Ray W.; Vestervej, Glostrup, Denmark

❦ The Song Worked! ❦

*W*hen we got engaged, my fiancé Rik lit-*erally counted down the days to our wedding. Since we were living in different cities at the time, it was very difficult to plan a wedding, but we stuck with it. The driver of the bus that Rik often took to work would always try to talk Rik out of getting married, even right up to the last few days before the wedding! It reminded us of Paul's song, "Ball and Chain." We've been married over seven years now, and that song remains just as special to us as it did when we were fixing to get married. Love really doesn't feel like a ball and chain to us!*

—Chrissie J.; Lafayette, California

"Ball and Chain"
was included on the album,
Heroes *released in 1990,*
along with these
additional songs:

If I Could Bottle This Up

Daddy's Come Around

Love Lives On

Heroes

I'm So Glad I Was Dreaming

Straight and Narrow

Billy Can't Read

She Supports Her Man

'Til the Mountains
Disappear

The Calm at the
Center of My Storm

(BMG Music; RCA Corporation)

Awards
1993 *CCMA*
Country Songwriter
of the Year

❧ In Sickness and in Health ❧

*M*y husband and I have been married for 16 years. There have been many years of struggle and pain associated with substance abuse and other destructive behaviors. One night, when I was out looking for my husband and feeling like I almost hated him, trying to figure out why on earth I was looking for him one more time—that's when your song, "Ball and Chain" came on the radio, and right then I realized why it was that I felt so upset: I still loved him…I didn't really hate **him**, but rather his alcoholism. That moment of insight and clarity helped me hang on to the shred of hope I needed to get through that crisis. There have been more difficult times since that night, but I no longer struggle with how I really feel. I know that, no matter whatever happens, I really do love my husband, in sickness and in health.

—Lucretia L.

The third strand is Jesus.

Chapter 15

Billy Can't Read

In my life, I have known some really brilliant people who were illiterate. They come up with all sorts of ways to compensate for their lack of reading ability. For instance, when they might go into a restaurant to eat, they'll order from the menu...but only the meals they see pictured on the menu. Unless something happens in their life to help them deal with the problem, they can become very creative and skillful at hiding the fact that they can't read.

When Jerry Michael and I got together to write this song, we thought of actual scenarios that we knew about...and even imagined some that we didn't really know about—but we never figured how close to real life we were getting! I recorded the song on the *Heroes* LP, my second album for *RCA Records.* I loved the song and wanted to

Verse One

His Mama and his Daddy
were very poor,

And they never
went to school;

Billy followed in their
footsteps, like a lot
of children do.

He had to get a job to
help pay the bills,

So his younger
brother, Ben,

Might go to school, and
learn to read and write,

And maybe he could
teach all of them.

Chorus One

(But) Billy can't read;
no, Billy can't read.

But he gives two
hundred percent

For the minimum
wage that he receives.

Sometimes he pretends
like he can as he looks

And he laughs at the
pictures in the
funny books;

But it really ain't funny,
you see, that Billy
can't read.

Verse Two

Then the boss man
came around

To talk to Billy one day;

He said, "Now, Billy,
you're the hardest
worker I've got,

And you sure deserve
more pay.

But the boss at the top
says I have to give

put it out as a single. The record company was against it—they didn't feel that radio would respond to a "cause song" in a positive way at that time. I just thought it would do a lot of good if it could be a single, but it didn't look like it was going to happen.

I performed the song on the *Nashville Now* TV show one night, and I had an immediate response. I got a call the next day from an organization called Literacy Volunteers of America (LVA). They wanted to use the song as their theme song. Later, I worked with them for awhile as a spokesperson. Then one day, the record company let me know they were going to release it as a single. It seems that *Country Music Television* and the *Country Music Association* both wanted to do something for the community, and had decided that literacy was the issue that they most wanted to address. They wanted to know if *RCA* would do a video and release a single on the song, "Billy Can't Read." I was thrilled!

When the video was made, we added a national hot line number—1-800-228-8813—at the end that people could call to get hooked up with their local LVA chapter…and they could learn to read! This was a tremendous success. Many adults learned to read because of this, and many people got involved, volunteering to teach those who couldn't read; even my mom in Mississippi volunteered. However, the record company was right: radio didn't love the song like I did, and it wasn't a big chart success. But it *was* one of the great highlights of my career.

Once, when I was taping a TV show about literacy in Tampa, Florida, I was fortunate to meet a 70-year old black lady who learned to read because of this song. She had three grown children who were all professionals—dentists, doctors, etc.—all established and successful in their careers. Yet she had taken in laundry and did ironing for people to put her children through college because she herself was illiterate. Her husband had passed away, and she had some time on her hands, so she entered the literacy program because, for one thing, she wanted to be able to write a check.

Later I heard about a man named Billy, who was interviewed on a TV news show. His life story paralleled the song—yet the song was written about a fictitious character! It seemed to me the Holy Spirit knew him...and He was involved in a big way when this song was written.

Letters

—➤•◄—

⇌ Inspired to Keep Trying ⇌

There are several songs on the Heroes *CD that touch my heart, but "Billy Can't Read" is the one that affects me the most. I am a special education teacher finishing my last year,*

Every foreman
a written test."

Billy hung his head
because he knew
right then,

That he'd always have to
settle for less.

Verse Three

Well, little Ben never
took for granted

All his brother, Billy,
sacrificed.

Every night, while the
family slept,

They would sit up late
by that old lamp light;

Sounding out the A's and
the E's and the I's,

And the O's and the U's;

And now he's reading
everything from his
cereal box,

To the Bible three times
through.

Chorus Two

Now Billy can read; yeah,
Billy can read.

And the rest of his life will
be different because

Of a special gift he
received.

Now he don't have to act
like he's laughing
as he looks

At the silly pictures in
those funny books;

They're as funny as
funny can be

Now that Billy can read.

His life is better, you see,

Now that Billy can read.

"Billy Can't Read"
by Paul Overstreet and
Jerry Michael. Scarlet Moon
Music (BMI) ~ Fifty Grand
Music, Inc. (BMI). 1990.

——⊰•⊱——

Awards
1994 *CCMA*
Mainstream Artist
of the Year

——⊰•⊱——

before I quit to stay home and start a family. The students I teach have been with me since they started middle school. I am very attached to them and feel responsible for their well-being. This is my last year to try and teach them to read before they go on to high school, and shortly thereafter, the real world. These kids are primarily self-contained and very limited in their skills, but I know if I can just teach them to read basic sight words and to sound most words out, their lives will be so much easier and enriched. The elation I sense and feel at the end of this song encourages me to keep trying, even in the face of defeating odds.

—**Peggy H.; Fulton, Missouri, USA**

❧ Six-Year Old "Teacher" ❧

All the songs on Paul Overstreet's [Best of Paul Overstreet] CD are special to my family, but one song in particular changed the way my six-year old daughter viewed the world. We were driving somewhere in the car and the song, "Billy Can't Read," came on the radio, and my daughter (who learned to read at age five) looked at me and asked how old "Billy" was. I told her I wasn't sure, but he was probably in his twenties. She immediately took on a look of concern and couldn't fathom the possibility of an adult not knowing how to read, when she herself—only six years old—could read everything. So she has taken it upon herself to teach everyone to read—her one-year old brother, the four-year old next door—whomever she can possibly teach, she does, because she wants everyone to enjoy the wonderful world of reading.

—Becky S.; Emmitsburg, Maryland

❧ A Real-Life "Billy" ❧

*M*y son, Paul, has a friend, Billy Delaney, who sounds very like "Billy" in this song. His father died suddenly when he was young, and Billy had to give up his studies to support the family. Eventually when the family was reared, Billy went back to college, and I'm delighted to say that he qualified as a dentist in 1998. He started his own first job in August as a dentist working for the Western Health Board in County Roscommon, Ireland. The song always brings a tear to my eyes when I think of both "Billy" in the song and "Billy the dentist." Keep up the good work.

—Peter O'B.; Ireland

About Paul Overstreet

Family—At the Heart of All He Does

Paul, his wife, Julie, and their six children—Nash, Summer, Chord, Harmony, Skye, and the latest addition, Charity Joy—plus an assorted pet menagerie, reside on a farm in a small town outside of Nashville.

Paul hits the trail in Elk Canyon, Colorado.

"Billy Can't Read"
was included on the album,
Heroes *released in 1990,*
along with these
additional songs:

Ball and Chain

If I Could Bottle This Up

Daddy's Come Around

Love Lives On

Heroes

I'm So Glad I Was Dreaming

Straight and Narrow

She Supports Her Man

'Til the Mountains
Disappear

The Calm at the
Center of My Storm

(BMG Music; RCA Corporation)

❧ From "Under" to "Over" ❧

*M*y son, Andre, has suffered from attention deficit disorder and the associated
learning disabilities for years. He struggled for
years with reading problems. I cannot begin to
explain how much the song, "Billy Can't
Read," meant to him. He would play it over
and over when he was little. He now reads
above grade level and is graduating from high
school a year early! I personally have too many
favorites to list. Paul's music has been an inspiration to my own life, as well as the lives of my
children. Paul has a God-given talent to touch
the heart and soul of all who listen to his
music. Thank you, Paul, for the inspiration and
years of wonderful and talented writing.

—**Kathleen V.; Warrenton, Oregon**

❧ She Wants to Learn ❧

*M*y seven-year-old daughter Nicole just loves
to hear "Billy Can't Read." She sings it at
the top of her lungs. She loves to read, and said
that she wants to be a first grade teacher when
she grows up so she can teach Billy to read. She
loves sounding out the A-E-I-O-U-s in the song.
When she gets discouraged, she reads her home-
work. I remind her that Billy was a grown man
before he could read, and that she didn't want to
be like that. It puts a new perspective on her
wanting to learn.

—**Marie C.; Prattsville, Alabama**

Chapter 16

What's Going Without Saying

This song started off because Jeff Borders told me a story from when he was first married. He was at a party with his wife—he said, "I looked across the room at her standing over there, and I thought to myself, 'I wonder if she knows that I think she's beautiful?' Then it dawned on me: how often do we let things go that we should be saying? I realized that I needed to tell her I think she is beautiful."

It really moved me deeply when he shared this with me. As we began writing this song, I recall how I felt like there was a guiding Presence bringing stories to mind that should be included in the lyrics. It was very hard to keep the emotions in check while writing. A lot of time, that's how I can tell when God is really involved in the composing of a song. On this song,

Verse One

He stood looking
at his father

Who was eighty-five
years old;

He remembered all
the ball games

They played so long ago.

Then he put his
arm around him,

And kissed him
on the cheek;

He said, "Dad, it's time
I told you

What a friend you've
been to me."

Chorus One

'Cause when you
love someone,

You got to let them know.

When you're thinking
of someone,

You need to tell them so.

Don't know what makes us
think our minds

And our hearts
can be read;

What's going without
saying should be said.

I sensed it was going have an impact…but I didn't really know how much until I played it for my wife. Julie just fell apart because it reminded her of her own father, who had passed away a long time ago. I think she can say it better than I, so I asked her to write about it for me:

Paul and I were driving down the road when he popped a new song that he'd just written into the tape deck and said, "Tell me what you think." Being married to Paul, I had heard so many great songs…but I wasn't prepared for where this one would take me. The song is basically about letting your loved ones know—while they're still here—that you love them.

Paul and Julie with their friends Colleen and Dennis Agajanean
in Sydney, Australia

Both of my parents died while I was still a teen. I never got to see them grow old...they never got to see me become a woman, a wife, a mother. Paul's song took me to that place I'd never been able to go before...and it was bittersweet. It made me miss them all over again and wish for the memories we never got to share...yet hearing this song was almost like being able to experience what it would have been like—that part I loved!

When I first heard this song, the tears started coming (which doesn't happen often). When the song ended, Paul looked at me and said, "So, what do you think?"—and, of course, I couldn't say anything! He just smiled, pushed the rewind button and played it again—he's a stinker that way!

There is one thing that too many people live with, an "evil" which can be entirely avoided: regret. The Bible is filled with examples of the principle of "sowing and reaping"—of encouraging people to be careful to plant little seeds of kindness that will later produce fruit of great love, joy, and kindness. Simple acts, things that don't take a lot of energy or time, or money, or even forethought...but which can transform a sad person's day into sunshine, or make a memory that will always be precious. "Whoever gives one of these

Verse Two

She stood in the doorway,

All grown up,
with children too;

Watching as her
Mama cooked

Just like she used to do.

She slowly walked
up to her,

And she held her
wrinkled hands;

She said, "So you know
you're the greatest Mom

A daughter ever had."

Verse Three

No one needs our roses

When the sun of life's
gone down;

If you're going to send a
message of your love,

Then send it now.

I don't believe
I've let you hear

The things you should
have heard;

I don't believe
I've truly put

My feelings into words.

'Cause to me, you are
so beautiful,

Much more than
words can say;

But if you don't mind
and you've got the time,

I'd like to try today.

Chorus Two

'Cause when you love
someone,

You got to let them know.

When you're thinking
of someone,

You need to tell them so.

My mind and my heart
can be read;

What's going
without saying,

What's going
without saying,

What's going without
saying should be said.

What's going without
saying should be said.

"What's Going Without
Saying" by Paul Overstreet
and Jeff Borders. Scarlet
Moon Music (BMI) South
Castle Songs (ASCAP). 1992.

little ones only a cup of cold water...
assuredly I say to you, he shall by no
means lose his reward" (Mt. 10:42).

Our lives follow the cycle of birth and
death, so it is inevitable that, eventually,
our loved ones will die and leave us or we
will leave them. So many people have told
me that this song really moved them to
speak to their loved ones while they still
have the chance. Don't let the chance pass
you by—tell someone you love them, and
if you need to, forgive them. Forgiveness
can set you free.

Letters

❧ A Good Start to Every Day ❧

*All of Paul's recordings are very inspira-
tional and help me to be a better person. I
play a Paul Overstreet CD every morning
before I start my day, and regardless of which
one it is, it serves to remind of something I
need to do that day to be a better person.
"What's Going Without Saying" reminds me
each day to tell those I love just what they mean
to me. It's so easy to forget to mention the
important things. Paul's music is good and
healthy, and the message in the lyrics are all so
decent, positive and very inspirational, so family-
oriented and from the heart.*

I think it would be so beneficial to the children of America if it were a requirement for them to begin each school day with any one of these recordings! It would help remind them "to do the right thing." I thank God for sending a man of Paul's caliber to this world we are living in today!

—Jennifer L.

❧ The Quilt of a Wonderful Life ❧

A few years ago, I heard a song called, "What's Going Without Saying." I loved that song at first "hear," and thought how profound those words were. Little did I know that they would come back to me over and over again, much as many Bible Scriptures do.

About four years ago, my very beloved grandmother was diagnosed with terminal cancer. I had always been close to my grandma; she taught me to read, to cook, to sew, to knit, to garden…and to be a generally nice person to others. She was just a wonderful woman to know. But for some reason—although we often said, "I love you"—we didn't sit there and go over all the things in our lives, saying how much we meant to one another. Instead, we usually tried to find ways to show our love and appreciation. Like her giving me my great-great-grandparents' hymnal, or sharing her world-famous bread recipe with me. I couldn't teach her anything because she had probably already lived it…so I tried to do things like getting her backstage to meet Vince Gill

"'What's Going Without Saying' reminds me each day to tell those I love just what they mean to me. It's so easy to forget to mention the important things."

Awards
"There But for the Grace of God Go I"
1994 Dove Award
Country Recorded
Song of the Year

"What's Going Without Saying"
was included on the album,
Love Is Strong released in
1992, along with these
additional songs:

Take Another Run

Still Out There Swinging

Me and My Baby

There But for the
Grace of God Go I

Love Is Strong

Head Over Heels

Take Some Action

Lord, She Sure Is Good
at Loving Me

'Til the Answer Comes

(BMG Music; RCA Corporation)

(whom she secretly had a crush on) (I was successful, by the way, and he was wonderful to her). Or I would bring the first blooms from my prize lavender rose bush.

About a month before she went to be with the Lord, I heard this song again. I just cried because I knew that I needed to go to her, to thank her for all she was to me, all she'd done for me—for always being there to listen to my joy, my sorrow, my pain, my excitement over some trivial thing that she could probably care less about but still jumped around with me over. I needed to tell her everything. So, with this song as my inspiration, I waited for the Lord to give me a time to go to her.

Two weeks later, I heard a still, small voice say, "Go, now." So I went. And I told her everything, just as I knew I should do. We both shared a lot of tears, a lot of memories, and it was a night that will live with me forever. Thank you for writing such a soul-baring, inspiring song that motivated me to ask God's guidance over this issue. It pulled together the "quilt of a wonderful life," where it rests warmly against my spirit.

—**Angela S.**

✎ A Lifetime Captured in Three Minutes ✎

My dad took a chance, and brought us as babies to Chicago, Illinois from Laredo, Texas. Living in small homes with few rooms and working the tomato fields every day, he brought us here to better our lives. He and my mom made sacrifices to give us a better opportunity at life through hard work and perseverance. There are seven children, with the youngest being my sister. I now own my own business, and instruct engineers all over the world how to be more productive with computer-aided engineering software. For my father's 70th birthday party, my sister and I will sing your song, "What's Going Without Saying," for him and my mother, to let them know how "beautiful" they are and "much more than words can say." We will also show a slide picture presentation of we children growing up, synchronized to "Seein' My Father in Me." The final frame will be my father. Thanks for the uncomplicated and sincerest of words, captured in three minutes, that describe a lifetime.

—Eduardo M.; Romeoville, Illinois

"It pulled together the 'quilt of a wonderful life,' where it rests warmly against my spirit."

Time for a four-wheeler ride with Dad

A labor of love

Chapter 17

'Til the Mountains Disappear

When Julie and I got married, we were so poor we couldn't even afford wedding rings. The day we planned to be married turned out to be the coldest day in Tennessee history. We went over to our pastor's house. The pipes had burst in his kitchen and he was kind of preoccupied with that, but he went on with the marriage ceremony as planned. Standing in his living room with his daughter as our witness, we repeated our vows and became man and wife. So we really didn't have a wedding with friends and family, so to speak.

As our third anniversary rolled around, my songwriting had started to find acceptance in the music industry, and I finally had a few dollars to spend on a diamond ring. A friend of mine told me about this diamond dealer, and I went and picked out a nice stone; then I picked out a ring setting and

Verse One

I have walked with my arm
around your shoulder,

I've placed a golden ring
upon your hand;

But now my heart is telling
me I should be bolder,

And take you to
the highest place

That you have ever been,

And say it all again.

Chorus One

I'll pledge my love to you
on the top of a mountain,

And I'll say it loud enough

for all the world to hear;

We'll let it echo through the deepest, darkest canyon,

And I'll be your companion 'til the mountains disappear.

Verse Two

The seasons will change down in the valley,

Like the heart of a fair-weather friend;

But if ever for one moment you should doubt me,

I will just start climbing through the snow

And through the wind, to say it all again.

Tag

Yes, I will be your companion

'Til the mountains disappear.

had it all put together. About this time, Tanya Tucker invited us to a Pro-Celebrity Ski Tournament in Steamboat Springs, Colorado—and I thought, "What a great place to celebrate our anniversary!"—so for our third anniversary, we went on a skiing holiday.

I didn't tell Julie, but I also asked our pastor if he could come out to Colorado and do the wedding ceremony again (to renew our vows). He loved to ski, so he agreed, and he and his wife flew out there…and I even managed to keep them hidden from Julie. On the day of our anniversary, I set it up with some friends that we would all go to the top of the mountain for hot chocolate—which was a little strange: all of us going up without our skis. When we got to the top of the gondola—right at the top of the mountain—there our pastor stood.

Julie realized right away what was going on. We walked out on this large deck, dressed in our ski clothes, and renewed our vows. With so many of our friends there, it was a fun time. I gave Julie the diamond ring that I had made for her, and she gave me this great pen, a gold Cross™, to write songs with.

That was a special day. When I returned home, I thought, "I've got to write a song about it." As Don Schlitz sat in our first writing appointment after our trip, we had a lot to talk about…but I didn't tell him about the ceremony at the top of the mountain until after we wrote and finished this song.

Recently, Julie and I were up in Banff, Alberta, Canada at a Family Life conference, and I was the guest singer for the first night. It was also supposed to be a "romantic" weekend for Julie and me—a getaway for us—but it got kind of busy and messed up. I had the chance to sing the night before in Minnesota, and we left early the next morning for Canada, so I was a little

Time out for a pose on the family ranch.

"'Til the Mountains
Disappear"
was included on the album,
Heroes *released in 1990,*
along with these
additional songs:

Ball and Chain

If I Could Bottle This Up

Daddy's Come Around

Love Lives On

Heroes

I'm So Glad I Was Dreaming

Straight and Narrow

Billy Can't Read

She Supports Her Man

The Calm at the
Center of My Storm

(BMG Music; RCA Corporation)

stressed out from singing and performing, and feeling a little tired. Julie kept wanting the emotional stuff from me that a husband is supposed to give on a weekend like this—she really had high expectations. I got angry, she got angry, and we were having a really tough weekend.

On Sunday morning, Dennis Rainey, the speaker, invited all the couples—in a room of only about 70 people, an intimate atmosphere—to stand up and renew their wedding vows. As Julie and I stood up, I was thinking, "Oh no, we have been arguing all weekend…and now here we are, standing up together, expected to say these things to each other that I can't find the feeling for inside." As Dennis started leading us in the vows, I was repeating after him exactly what he was saying…but it wasn't coming from my heart. As I looked into Julie's eyes, she had this "You don't mean a thing you're saying!" look on her face, and I couldn't blame her.

My mom had always told me that I had my emotions upside down. Sometimes I used to get tickled in church…and I couldn't stop laughing until Mom would have to take me outside and give me a good talking-to on the seat of my pants! Or when she and my stepfather were giving us a real stern "layin' the law down" conversation, I don't know why but I would just lose it. Well, here I was—at a so-called romantic weekend with my wife…in an intimate, church-like setting…with people all around at this solemn, tender moment, watching us—and I started getting that old silly feeling again.

I really did fight it hard! I made it all the way through my vows, thinking, "I hope I'll make it without totally disrupting this special moment for all the other couples." But then it was Julie's turn to be on the spot. She was doing fine, when all of a sudden she could see what was happening to me. I was right on the edge of hilarity. She told me later she was thinking, "Oh no, he is not going to do this here!"

When she got to the words, "for better or for worse," it sure sounded to me like she said "Worse!" a lot louder than she said the word "better." At that point, it was all over for me. I began to break out in a sweat. I just could not stop myself…I began laughing. Julie was helpless standing there, trying to finish her vows. She couldn't do it—she started laughing…and the next thing we knew, we were both hysterical.

I hung my head, hoping no one could tell if I was laughing or crying. Wouldn't you know it, but when the vows were ended, some guy came up, patted me on the back and asked, "Were you weeping?" I answered, "Yeah, that was it"—I was laughing so hard I was crying.

That's where it broke for us that weekend. All our expectations came down, and we were just real people after that, and

"Laugh together every chance you get—it's one of God's key healing tools: 'A merry heart does good, like medicine' (Prov. 17:22a)."

Awards
1994 *The Nashville Network*/*Music City News* Christian Country Artist of the Year

"...after listening to [your] song about 'going to the mountain top to show his love,' he took me to the tallest place here—and believe me, that was awesome—and he asked me to marry him."

really enjoyed each other. It's a good thing we had that other time when we renewed our vows to look back on, because this one didn't go so well!

Marriage has its ups and downs. It isn't always the way we want it to be, and that's why commitment is so important. Commitment carries you over the rough spots—you know, those places you come to when you don't have "that feeling" you once had, and you wonder if it will ever return. Well, take it from one who has been there—it does. Emotions come and go over time—but they can't be all that love and a marriage is about. It's much more than that. Remember: *"For better, for worse; for richer, for poorer; in sickness and in health; to love and to cherish; until death."* Love is all about going through it all together. Laugh together every chance you get—it's one of God's key healing tools: "A merry heart does good, like medicine" (Prov. 17:22a).

Letters

≈ **Love on a Mountaintop** ≈

*T*hank you for being faithful to the Lord. He has blessed you with so much. I am a woman who had been betrayed many times by her husband. Finally—after he decided to go away and "become a woman" and follow that *lifestyle—I was divorced. One day, I met this wonderful man who could see all the hurts and scars left on my heart. He decided that he loved me so much...but it was so hard for me to believe that. Then, after listening to [your] song about "going to the mountain top to show his love," he took me to the tallest place here—and believe me, that was awesome—and he asked me to marry him. It was so wonderful because he took me to the highest place I had ever been, and asked me to love him. What girl could resist that? It also is a place I will be able to see from our new house, when we get it built. We have been married now for over two years, and he is often pointing to that high place for me, reminding me of that time and that he still intends to keep his vow. I love that song, and he has sung it to me. Thank you so much.*

—**Connie K.**

"It was so wonderful because he took me to the highest place I had ever been, and asked me to love him."

Harmony and Chord strike a chord of true harmony.

Baby Charity plows the "back forty."

Chapter 18

One in a Million

While our family was vacationing and visiting with a good friend of mine, Joe White, who runs the Kanakuk summer camps for kids in Branson, Missouri, we met a lot of high school and college-aged kids. The camp goes around the country recruiting college girls and guys to counsel at the camp during the summer. Some of the girls would baby-sit for Julie and me every now and then, so we could have a little time to do some things by ourselves. We also had several conversations with them—especially the girls—that revealed a side of life of which I was not aware.

These great kids had committed to keeping themselves pure until their wedding day. I thought they would be getting all kinds of support from their peers, but I learned it was quite the opposite. They

Verse One

She gets all dressed up

And goes out
with her friends,

But she always goes home

When the party ends.

They tell her,
"Get with it, girl,

Life is passing you up."

But they all wish they
could be like her,

Still saving her love.

Chorus One

She's one in a million,

Waiting for one
in a million.

Someone will come
along one day and
take her hand;

Someone who's been
through all that she's
been through.

She's one in a million,

Waiting for her one in a
million kind of man.

were made fun of, and always received counsel in the *other* direction—even from adults, but especially from their peers. I knew then they were up against a tough battle. I guess we just never know what people are going through.

Out of those conversations, there was a desire birthed in me to write a song of encouragement to all of the girls and guys around the globe. There is incredible peer pressure in society—in schools, on TV, in movies, in music—to be sexually active. I guess I should have known there wouldn't be much support in that area because I never found any when I was growing up. The guys made fun of those (boys or girls) who were virgins. I remember having a heart for keeping myself pure until I got

Daddy's "one in a million" girls

married. I also remember making the mistake of sharing that with a couple of guys…and they let me know how stupid they thought that was!

We really need to be there for our kids, to talk with them all the way through those high-pressure years. If you are "One in a Million" who has stayed sexually pure, I want you to know I'm proud of you.

Letters

❧ "Pick-Me-Up" and "Dance-With-Me" ❧

I can't honestly say the one of Paul Overstreet's songs has affected my life; it was one of his masterpieces, however, that got me hooked on Country music: "Forever and Ever, Amen." After that, I just couldn't get enough of his music. I picked up every record I could find that had one of his tunes on it. Boy, was I in heaven when he actually released a record of his own, "Sowin' Love."

Over the years, Paul's music has been the "pick-me-up" in the bad times, and the "dance-with-me" in the good times. I've met Paul on several occasions, and have found the man to be as much of an inspiration as his music. He has always made me feel like one of the family, not just a fan.

Verse Two

She wrote in her diary

About a boy named John,

But he felt he couldn't wait,

And now his golden chance is gone.

She's felt the hunger and the desire;

But she is going to wait until

It's time to burn that fire.

Tag

She's not in a hurry

To lose what she can never have again.

"One in a Million" by Paul Overstreet and Tom Campbell. Scarlet Moon Music (BMI) 1995.

"One in a Million"
was included on the album,
Time released in 1996,
along with these
additional songs:

We've Got to Keep on
Meeting Like This

I'm Gonna Ring Her

Even When It Don't
Feel Like It

Let's Go to Bed Early

You Gave Me Time

I Always Will

Blackberry Cobbler

Mr. Miller

My Rock

Scarlet Moon Records)

If I had to pick only one song that I related to and made me feel it was okay to be me, I'd have to say it's "One in a Million." I've lived my whole life feeling that I was different from everyone else because of choices I've made and the standards I've set. "Million" made me realize that I am indeed unique, but that's not such a bad thing after all!

—**Sheila H.; Ellington, Connecticut**

✏ Waiting for Her One-in-a-Million ✏

A lot of your songs have touched me, but my favorite is "One in a Million." I really identify with the woman in that song. I am 33 years old and I am yet to find my "one in a million." I am a member of the Church of Jesus Christ of Latter Day Saints, but live in a small town where there's not a lot of singles. However, when I hear your song, it renews my faith. I know that if it's the Lord's will, I will have that "one in a million" someday. Thank you for your music, and especially that song.

—**Tammy F.**

✏ Encouraged by Song ✏

The song, "One in a Million" touches me at the heart. I am a 17-year old girl and feel the pressure of sex before marriage. But I have promised myself and whoever I marry that I will save myself. This song really encouraged me.

—**Marilyn S.; Perth, Western Australia**

❧ Gentleness and Meekness ❧

I've been listening to Paul Overstreet since I was a pre-teen. Whenever I needed to feel at peace with God and refuel, I go to Paul's music. It is evident in the lyrics and tunes that God Himself inspires him, and that His Holy Spirit is present in his daily walk and in his music. His music has a gentleness and meekness, not puffed up or proud. You can see the very countenance of Christ in his eyes on his record covers and videos. I can't begin to tell you how many times his music has brought the power of the Omnipotent into my soul, and refreshed, encouraged, calmed, and strengthened my entire being.

Some of the songs, like, "One in a Million," speak directly to me, but all speak to me in one way or another. Paul Overstreet is the biggest blessing Country music ever received, and I thank God there are people out there still willing to set an example of godly humility and charity. God bless.

—**Heather M.**

Skye gives Daddy a little sugar for his jaw.

> *"Whenever I needed to feel at peace with God and refuel, I go to Paul's music. It is evident in the lyrics and tunes that God Himself inspires him, and that His Holy Spirit is present in his daily walk and in his music."*

Chapter 19

The Day My Daddy Didn't Come Home

This may be the toughest song I've ever written. As Alan Shamblin and I began working on this, it was tough not to let it get to me. I know now it has touched several people who have a similar history as mine, which seems to be far too common in our world. There is always more to a story than you will hear from one side, so you have to bear that in mind as you read this or listen to the song.

My father preached in a small country church. There were five kids in our family; I was the youngest. A country preacher just doesn't get enough financial support from a small church like that, so I guess that's why Daddy took whatever kind of work he could during the week. It had to be a job that didn't require him to work on Sundays, and would still give him time to prepare to preach.

Verse One

I waited for the sound
of his old truck

Pulling in the driveway,

But it never did show up
on that fateful Friday.

Darkness fell,
and I went inside;

I remember it all so clear;

There my Mama sat
with a goodbye letter,

In a pool of tears.

That was the day
everything started
going wrong,

The day my Daddy didn't
come home.

Chorus

He was somewhere on the
road to California,

Where the palm trees
sway,

And the weather's
always fine;

He had a new love
by his side,

But let me warn you;

He sure left some
broken-hearted folks
behind.

Verse Two

From that day on,
everything was different;

I played ball, but he was
never in the stands.

Mom remarried, but who
on Earth could blame her;

But I never really was
his little man.

It was the saddest day
my life had ever known,

The day my Daddy
didn't come home.

I don't know for sure what all was going on at home, or what my dad and mom were going through in their relationship at the time—I was too young to really understand. Kids just know that it feels good to have both parents there. Anyway, Dad was driving a milk truck for a company called *Sealtest*, delivering milk to different grocery stores on the Gulf Coast of Mississippi. It was during this time that he met a woman who worked at one of the stores. They started up a relationship that soon led to the separation and eventual divorce of my parents. I wasn't sure what was going on—I just knew that one day, my dad was there...and the next day, he just didn't come home. He was gone with this other woman, and had moved to California (she became his second wife).

The hardest part of that day for me was watching my mom cry, and seeing what my brothers and sisters were going through. I was too young to know what the impact would be on me then, but I think the hardest part for me was in the years ahead, growing up without my dad around. I loved sports—baseball, basketball, football, and a lot of things that boys like to do with their dads—but my dad never got to come to any of my games (that I can remember).

Looking back, it didn't seem like a long time before my mom and dad were both remarried. I went back and forth between them some, but I mostly stayed with my mom. When Mom remarried, my stepfather already had three children, and the children on both sides of the event were not happy at all. I can't say that there was anything intentional, but that made it rough.

My stepfather was a good man, but he was not without problems of his own. However, he tried to take care of my mom, and they did pretty well for several years. He was a hard worker, made good money, and tried to help with the kids—and I have to give him credit for that. I remember that he took Mom and me to see *Your Cheatin' Heart* (the movie about the life and career of Country music superstar Hank Williams), and on the ride home, I told them, "That's what I'm going to do, write songs." Also on that ride home, I wrote a song called "My Daddy Was a Preacher"— it wasn't very good, but it was the first one I can remember writing.

Mom and my stepfather kept us younger children going to church; I know it was more from Mom, but he went too. He had two sons of his own, and I was kind of an extra around a lot of the time. I guess it was a good thing that my stepfather was there to provide for my mom and the family in the early years, but the way it all ended was no pretty picture.

I really missed my daddy. It would not have mattered to me if we were rich or

Bridge

Now darling, I know
you and I have had
our struggles,

Sometimes we both
wanted to leave and
not come back

Some say our kids are
strong, and in time
they'd recover;

But I'm still not over that.

Well, it's been long
enough.

The greatest argument I've
got for holding on

was the day my Daddy
didn't come home.

"The Day My Daddy
Didn't Come Home"
by Paul Overstreet and
Alan Shamblin.
2000.

"It would not have mattered to me if we were rich or poor— I just wanted my dad around."

poor—I just wanted my dad around. Just having our family together would have been a great thing, but that's not the way it was—so we deal with it, we grow up and move on. But we will always carry the scars of it, and we will respond to many things in life in different ways because of it. Divorce is not a pretty thing for anybody. It should not be seen as a simple solution to marital problems, especially if there are children, since it usually brings about many more problems than it solves. The Bible says that God hates divorce (see Mal. 2:16)—that should tell us something! One thing I know for sure is that God can use anything for good.

I know it really takes commitment to make a marriage last forever. That's the

Boating at Table Rock Lake—Paul and Chord.

resolve I have for myself, my wife, our kids: to have a commitment that will carry us through the rough times. It isn't always easy, just like this song says. There are times we want to quit and walk away, but there's too much at stake. As our kids get older, it becomes different every day. Just when we get used to one stage, it all changes and we're faced with new challenges.

As I've played this song live, I have seen the impact that divorce has left both on the children and on those who have left their families. And I've had successfully married couples tell me, "There were times when we talked about calling it off, ending the marriage. But now—how wonderful it is when the grandkids come over, how important that relationship is…and we might have missed all that if we had not held onto each other and to the marriage! We love each other so much now."

This is not to say that people who have been divorced and remarried can't rebuild their lives. I was briefly married and divorced eight years before I met Julie. I had been praying for a wife—and then I met Julie. We talked about marriage, but I started to get those same old fears again—I still didn't feel like I was strong enough to do it again. When I revealed this to Julie, she got these big old tears in her eyes, and in a soft voice said, "We'll just have to pray that we love each other more every day." That's when I felt God

"The Day My Daddy Didn't Come Home"

Even though this song has never been released, it was included in the book because of its great popularity. A demo version of the song was produced, but it has yet to be released to the public. Paul has sung this song in many of his concerts across the country and its words have found a place in the hearts of thousands who quickly identify with its message.

"Mr. Overstreet, I love all of your songs, but 'The Day My Daddy Didn't Come Home' really stands out to me. I believe it's where we come from and the things we learn that mold our future."

begin to work on my heart—I was about to reject the gift that God was trying to give to me!—that was when a comfort and peace came over me.

God has brought so many blessings into my life because of Julie. We have been married now for 16 years, and have 6 wonderful children. I'm committed to seeing it through all the way to the finish line.

Letters

"Daddy's Little Girl"

Mr. Overstreet, I love all of your songs, but "The Day My Daddy Didn't Come Home" really stands out to me. I believe it's where we come from and the things we learn that mold our future. My father left my mom, my two brothers and me when I was three. I was devastated. I was "Daddy's little girl." Mama said I was a lot like him. He had a beautiful voice, and I guess you could say we had at least that in common.

Mama was born in Memphis, Tennessee, and I get my Country side from her. Being raised by her alone, I was reared on Country music, and have been in several Country bands; to this day, I am still performing my music. As a child, I too remember standing in the welfare line, waiting for food stamps. Mama hated doing that, but we had food on the table. She always worked two jobs to support us. She used to come home tired and say, "Baby, sing Mama a song"—that would calm her after a hard day's work. If our daddy hadn't left us, it would not have been that way.

A couple of years ago, we were sitting at her house, and she looked at me and said, "I don't know what I would do if I could never hear your voice anymore." I was touched. Then last year, she was killed in an automobile accident. I guess now I know what she meant about never hearing my voice again because, even though Mama couldn't hold a tune, I miss her voice every day. But growing up without anything makes you appreciate life more as an adult.

I think you have done a fine job with yours, Mr. Overstreet. Thank you.

—Tricia K.; Shreveport, Louisiana

❧ Effective Deterrent ❧

Several years ago, I fell away from my Christian walk and back into the life extolled in most Country music. I was just about ready to leave my beautiful family when I heard "The Day My Daddy Didn't Come Home" and some of your other songs. It brought me back home, where I happily am today. Thank you for what your music has done for me.

—Doug R.; Tulsa, Oklahoma

> "I was just about ready to leave my beautiful family when I heard 'The Day My Daddy Didn't Come Home' and some of your other songs. It brought me back home, where I happily am today."

———◆———

Chapter 20

God Is Good (All the Time)

Don Moen of *Integrity Music* had been talking with me about doing something Country for his upcoming album, *Rivers of Joy*. Don and I had become friends while I was producing a Susie Luchsinger album for them. We had a lot in common…at that time, we both had five children—now I have surpassed him on that! We were also discussing the possibility of me recording an album for *Integrity Music,* which I later did, titled *Time*. It was during this time that we began to write the song, "God Is Good (All the Time)."

I had been in the habit of taking my children to Colorado each winter to snow-ski. Don was a skier, and so were his wife and children, so we made a plan to go to Steamboat Springs, Colorado, together. While there, we decided to write something for his record, which turned out to be a great

Chorus

God is good all the time;

He put a song of praise in this heart of mine.

God is good all the time;

Through the darkest night, His light will shine.

God is good, God is good all the time.

Verse One

If you're walking through the valley,

There are shadows all around;

Do not fear,
He will guide you,

He will keep you
safe and sound.

He has promised to
never leave you,

Or forsake you, and
His Word is true.

Verse Two

We were sinners
and so unworthy;

Still for us He chose to die.

Filled us with
His Holy Spirit;

Now we can
stand and testify

That His love is
everlasting,

And His mercies,
they will never end.

Bridge

Though I may not
understand

All the plans You
have for me,

plan and a great time, building a friendship between he and I and our families.

One day instead of skiing, Don and I buckled down to work on the song which became "God Is Good." It was very challenging to say all the things that we wanted to say about how God is good…and at the same time, think about those who might be sitting out there with things going haywire in their lives. How did we say to someone who was walking through the toughest times—someone who had no history with God's goodness—that "God is good all the time"? We knew we couldn't just throw out a bunch of flowery lyrics and that would be it—we worked very hard at writing in a way that acknowledged the fact that you may be at a time when you're going through the valley, but God will be there with you.

Don later shared this true, heart-wrenching story with me:

Eight young people and four adults traveled to a remote lake in the Canadian wilderness for a spiritual retreat and fishing trip. All week long, they had been singing, 'God Is Good (All the Time)' as a theme song for their retreat. Late one night, after a wonderful time of fishing and fellowship around a campfire, they got in their boats to travel back to the cabin on the other side of the lake. A storm came up suddenly, and before they could paddle to shore, heavy waves and strong winds capsized their canoe and the two boats they had been in. As they were clinging to the boats in the icy 29-degree water, they sang the song they had been singing all week, 'God Is Good (All the Time),' and committed their lives to their Creator. Out of the twelve, only four survived—but they were able to face death without fear.

I know the song has done a tremendous work around the world. I hear stories about it being sung in many foreign countries. I'm thrilled to be a part of a song that has had that kind of impact, and I'm thankful that Don made that trip to Colorado to slave over the keyboards with so much snow out there beckoning on the ground!

My life is in Your hands;

And through the eyes of faith

I can clearly see.

Ending

God is good, He's so good all the time.

"God Is Good (All the Time)" by Paul Overstreet and Don Moen. Integrity's *Hosanna!* Music/ASCAP Scarlet Moon Music/BMI. 1999.

Paul with his co-writer and producer.

"God is Good"
was included on the album,
Living by the Book
released in 2000, along
with these additional songs:

Lost and Found

He Is Risen

Dig Another Well

Everybody Needs Your Touch

Living by the Book

Steady Working

Oh Why

I Will Carry My
Cross for You

Until We Know

Heart of My Heart

Wise Men Still Seek Him

I Won't Take Less
Than Your Love

(Scarlet Moon Records)

Letters

❧ One Sunday Morning... ❧

*J*uly 28, 1998 started out like most other days for me, except that I was going to have breakfast with my favorite cousin and his father. My husband had told me that my cousin and uncle were in town but would be leaving the next morning, so if I wanted to see them, I would have to be at my parents' house by 7:30 a.m. Although I got home from my night-shift job at 3:15 a.m., I was still there to talk, laugh, reminisce, and have a wonderful time with my cousin. About 10:00 a.m., my cousin said he had to be going, so they got in his pickup truck and headed toward the east coast of Florida, to my uncle's house. Their plan was for my cousin to spend several days there doing errands for his dad, then go on home to Atlanta.

Later that day, I had a message delivered to me at work at 10:45 p.m., telling me to call home as soon as possible. I was prepared to hear that perhaps one of my elderly parents had passed away—but I was not ready to hear that my 53-year-old cousin had experienced a massive coronary and was dead. I was in shock. Three months later, my dad found my mother dead in their home. Three months later, my very favorite aunt died from cancer. Three months after that, my dad died. Between those deaths were nine other close friends' deaths. I was numb when Dad died on Easter Sunday 1999, but was glad he was released from his earthly suffering. What a beautiful day to go and be with our Heavenly Father...and his bride of 62 years.

I have suffered from depression, not severe, for years, but all this seemed to push me over the edge. I took a leave of absence from my job, and tried to take care of my dad's estate. But I was not able to function without my husband with me; he was so loving and patient with me. One Sunday morning, he asked me if I had ever listened to our favorite Country radio station on Sundays and heard a program called, "Rise Up." I had not. So, just to humor him, I started listening, thinking something had to be out there to help me. That's when I heard your song, "God Is Good (All the Time)," I cried. It was like a sign from God to me that I would be alright and would be able to go on with my life.

I heard that song again this morning, on my way to work, and it meant so much to me. I am now working the day shift instead of night, but I don't get to attend our church very often because of conflicts in the church worship schedule and my work schedule. When I got to work this morning, everyone asked me why I was in such a good mood—I told them it was because I had heard this wonderful song and it really filled me with the Spirit. I have reached a turning point in my life, and I know that, with God's help, I am going to keep on going.

—Mary Anne N.; Seminole, Florida

"...when I heard your song, 'God Is Good (All the Time),' I cried. It was like a sign from God to me that I would be alright and would be able to go on with my life."

"...among the crowd were two teens who had appointments for abortions the next week. After seeing us perform this routine—with the message that was sent through the words of the song—there were two lives saved as a result."

❧ God's Heart ❧

Although I've only heard a couple of the praise songs Paul has written, I have to say that "God Is Good (All the Time)" is my favorite! I first heard it during an evangelical medical missions trip to the Philippines. One Sunday we joined worship with a large church in Olongapo City; that song was part of their worship set, and I fell in love with it immediately. The congregation praised God with such joy when singing it, and it was very exciting. As soon as our mission team returned to our church in Okinawa, Japan, we adopted that song into our worship team as well. The church loved it and always got excited proclaiming those words. I appreciated the song even more when I finally heard it performed by Paul and Don Moen on one of the Hosanna! Worship *CDs. I look forward to hearing that song and others on the* Living by the Book *CD. Paul, you really seem to have captured God's heart in your music!*

—**Mark H.; Okinawa, Japan**

❧ Life-Saving Song ❧

A few years back, our church dance team started dancing to a song called "God Is Good." We decided to perform it for the Boone crisis pregnancy center. While there, among the crowd were two teens who had appointments for abortions the next week. After seeing us perform this routine—with the message that was sent through the words of the song—

there were two lives saved as a result. The teens cancelled their appointments, and now each of them have a healthy baby to care for. We always dedicate this dance routine to the Lord, believing that someone else might get a positive message from this song. I just want to let you know what a fantastic message you are sending to people. I'm glad to see you with Franklin Graham. Keep up the good work.

—Stephanie R.; Boone, North Carolina

∽ Different Flavors— Same Message of Hope ∽

I don't profess to be a Country music fan, but when I heard "God Is Good" by Don Moen and Paul Overstreet, the sheer joy and God's love that is in this song jumped out at me. The whole excellent production of that song just sparkles with vitality and hope, putting God in His rightful Number One Priority place, even when things are dark and difficult around us. I have heard this song in various countries around the world—and whether it's sung with an Eastern European accent, an Australian flavor or an African beat, it still has the same consistent encouragement every time.

—Michele G.; Littleton, Colorado

"I don't profess to be a Country music fan, but when I heard 'God Is Good' by Don Moen and Paul Overstreet, the sheer joy and God's love that is in this song jumped out at me."

More "Fan Mail"

Hundreds of e-mails and letters were received when Paul put out a general call for comments…and their tributes could put a saint to shame! But our purpose is here to let the "fans" have their say, so here is a further sampling of what people wrote about Paul Overstreet and his songs:

✎ A Great Family Guy ✎

I grew up in Nashville in the 1960s with Country music, and was a big fan then. I became a Christian in my early twenties, and got away from the music because of the message it was presenting. I can't pick a special song as I thoroughly enjoy them all, along with my entire family. It is something to get four teenagers and my wife and I to all agree on the music we like. I really enjoy the music and especially the message that accompanies it. I had the opportunity to meet Paul twice—once, at the Governor's Prayer Breakfast; and another time when returning from Korea on a business trip. He is a great family guy and a heart for God! Praise the Lord! Hope to hear many more new songs.

—**David L., Springfield, Tennessee**

✎ Paul's Kickin' Tunes ✎

What an encouragement your lyrics and music have been. From the first song until now, I have enjoyed every song on every album. It started over a decade ago when I was a university student, tree-planting way up north. The crew were all new to me, but the common bond that broke the ice was this Paul Overstreet CD. I came to realize there were other brothers in the Lord on the crew. After a long day of trudging and planting in the bush, warding off black flies, Paul's music would bring us back to life, and then lull us all to sleep. Since then, I have enjoyed every album and have given them as gifts. Our days at Campus Crusade were highlighted by line-dancing house parties and some square dances that always included kickin' Paul tunes. He has been blessed by the Lord, and has been a blessing to me. Praise the Lord from whom all blessings flow.

—**Ian B.**

❧ Touched Heart, Body and Soul ❧

How could I or anyone pick a song and then say this one touched me? It would be easier and more correct to say Paul Overstreet has never written a song that didn't touch me. I myself write and sing, went to Nashville in the early 1970s, was offered a contract with a record company. But I wouldn't leave my kids behind, and my wife at that time didn't believe in my dream. Many times when I sing one of my songs, my style of writing has been compared to yours. All I say is thanks, and I wish I could write a song that touches the heart, body and soul the way Paul Overstreet can. To me, you are the best...any one of your songs will touch some area of the one who hears it. So keep doing what you do best— touching us with your music, and we'll keep on enjoying being touched by it!

—**Rusty C.**

❧ Fundamental Truths ❧

Almost every song that Paul Overstreet has put out has touched a part of my life. I am from Morton, a small town west of Newton, Mississippi. Like many displaced Mississippians, I used my God-given talents to leave the state and pursue a "better" life. I have spent all of my adult life working in the computer field, surrounded by people who do not understand from where I come. The daily stress caused by miscommunications and different priorities take a heavy toll. When this old world gets me down, I listen to a few of Paul's songs, and the pressures are put into their proper perspective and I am once again on the path. Paul's music expresses the fundamental truths that I learned from my family in Missis-sippi—FAMILY, work hard every day, "dig another well," and help others. This is the antithesis of today's world that preaches, "Live hard, drive fast, leave a beau-tiful corpse." An online reviewer once lamented that "Paul's 'Christian' music would have you believe that going home to your wife would be better than drink-ing with your friends." But I say, "Keep singing, Mr. Overstreet; they have the words right but they have not yet learned the lessons." In the meantime, I will be immensely entertained and will eagerly wait for each new release.

—James T.

✎ Music Spoke Right to Heart And Soul ✎

I cannot begin to express what your music has meant to me and my family. I began listening to your music around 1994, when a fellow Christian friend at work told me about you. I was struggling with many issues in my life and facing many challenges…I was at a very low point. Your music—although classified as Country—contained such strong morals and spoke right to my mind and soul. It contained much wit and wisdom that my father had raised me with. However, with all the hustle and bustle of life, with the struggles added on top, it is so easy to lose focus.

I never understood the term "backsliding." For me, it's always been more like free-falling. I believe I have been greatly blessed through your music, and still find it all as a source of strength and comfort. Thank you. God has blessed not only me, but many others through your efforts. Please continue to write. I know you have many people who are blessed by God through your music. I pray for you and your family, and pray that God continues to lead you to write, and that you respond to Him. God bless.

—**Mark D.; New Orleans, Louisiana**

✎ Songs Reflect Realities and Rewards of Relationships ✎

*I*t's amazing how many of Paul's songs have enhanced and reflected various aspects of my life, especially my marriage, fatherhood and respect for my par-ents. "Lord, She Sure Is Good at Loving Me"…"All the Fun"…"'Til the Mountains

Disappear"..."I Always Will"..."Richest Man on Earth" and many others have reminded me how sweet life is (and always can be) with the woman God chose for me. Those songs have helped me appreciate the value of my sweet, humble and fun-loving wife, who knows what it means to keep romance alive while still honoring God above all things. Songs like "Sowin' Love"..."Seein' My Father in Me"..."Heroes" and others have enhanced the deep love and respect I feel for my parents, in addition to how I feel in my role as Daddy to my three wonderful daughters. Paul's songs reflect the realities and rewards of these important relationships, the hope in overcoming obstacles, and how all things can be enjoyed in light of God's love. Paul also shows that life as a Christian can be fun and even romantic, while still showing reverence and love for the Creator of it all. Thank you, Paul, for your inspiration! May God continue to bless you abundantly in your own marriage, ministry, career, and all you put your hand to.

—Mark H.; San Antonio, Texas

✑ Antidote to Media Bombardment ✑

It would be hard for me to pick just one song. I have received hope, encouragement, inspiration, and an example of what a Christian marriage and family could be like from many of your songs. I grew up in a broken home, where everyone was out for themselves. There was abuse at worst and dysfunction at best. When I was saved by Jesus at the age of 12, I began to dream of someday getting married and being a mother, and having [a] family of my own where I could break the cycle of destruction in my family. But I knew very few Christian men. I was afraid I would not be able to find a man who would love me as Christ loved the Church, a man who would be faithful and not hurt me or his children. I began listening to your music, and realized that there are men out there like that. It gave me a standard with which to compare the men I dated.

God answered my prayers when I met my husband, Michael. We have been married for almost six years now and have two children. It has not always been easy. We both have had to let go of a lot of baggage from the past, and I have had health problems which have made intimacy in our marriage difficult and left my husband with the responsibility of work and the home at times. When I get discouraged, I listen to "Straight and Narrow" or "The Calm at the Center of My Storm." When I feel unimportant, I can listen to "Love Lives On" and "Heroes."

When I feel unlovable, my husband will play "If I Could Bottle This Up" and "'Til the Mountains Disappear" for me.

I feel so blessed to be able to change the legacy of my family for my children...that my daughter will have an example of a man after God's own heart for a father, and my son will grow to see how to love his wife and children and be their spiritual leader. In a day when children are bombarded with media and music that rejects God's will for the home, it is nice to hear them singing along with your music. Thank you for the blessings your music has given me and my family. I pray that God will continue to use you as a vessel with which to show His will for families, and offer encouragement for those who are seeking His will in their lives.

—**Brandy M.**

A Mother's Role

I think "Merry Christmas, Mary" is the prettiest Christmas song ever. In this song, Mary is recognized for her part in the wonderful birth of Christ. I'm not a feminist by a long means, but mothers and their role in children's lives are often swept under the rug. The joy that must have been in her heart when this special but mysterious Child was born needs a special recognition. Thanks for writing and singing this wonderful song!

—**Sandy W.**

Country-Born Wisdom

My husband and I are Christians who love Country music. After having gone through painful divorces with our former spouses, leaving us for each other, Ken and I found hope and healing with the Lord's strength. Paul's music was instrumental in restoring in us hope and joy in God's real plan and purpose for family and marriage. The Lord gave us a second chance at love as He intended. During our courtship, we spent many days and evenings listening to the country-born wisdom of Paul Overstreet. Some of our favorites include "All the Fun"..."Love Never Sleeps"..."Keep On Meeting Like This" and the recessional at our wedding, "What God Has Joined Together." Life had given us "dirt" thrown in our well...but we rejoiced as we heeded the advice of "old Ike" and dug another well! We happily celebrated our first anniversary on June 5, 2000!

—**Kendra D.; Lake Forest, California**

⚮ Marriage Saver ⚮

I *have loved good Country music for many years; really, I can't say a lifetime or anything for I am only 24 years old. To be quite honest, I didn't really know of you. I knew all the songs that others had sang—I just didn't know they were written by you. I first got to know you in June 2000. My husband and I attended an "I Still Do" event in Denver, Colorado. Immediately I was curious about your lifestyle; I mean, you were singing at a Christian marriage event…and you were a Country singer. I had struggled with the idea of whether I should give up listening to Country music at all, trying to be a godly woman. Then to have a Country entertainer at this event was a shock. But immediately I loved your music, and enjoyed your show completely. I did buy the "I Still Do" CD at the end of the day, but my CD player at home was broken so it stayed wrapped up for a month. Today, I opened it and listened to the song, "I Still Do"…and cried the whole way through.*

I married my husband at 18 years old. I had not yet even graduated from high school. My parents separated at the beginning of April and I married at the end of April, all in the same year. I have struggled so much of my marriage with the idea of divorce. Things were not easy when you marry at 18 and try to grow up and mature inside this covenant called marriage. My husband was only 21. In the first five years of marriage, we moved ten times and had three children. We were exhausted and stressed…and not just the financial stress of being a stay-at-home mom, surviving on one income. We wanted to have a godly marriage and be godly parents, but sometimes in the midst of all we've done, it is easy to forget why we committed in the first place. We became like roommates, trying to survive the small babies and empty checking account. I was tempted daily to leave and give it all up. To be honest, my husband adores me and our three daughters. He is committed to me—but in my heart, I wasn't to him. So we planned to attend an "I Still Do" event in February 2000, but didn't.

However, in May 2000, we attended a high school reunion…and there at the reunion was a young man I had loved fiercely in high school. We visited many times throughout the evening—there was a connection between our hearts. It had always been there; he was probably the only person I had ever truly given myself to. I loved him so much…and I went home with these feelings. I hadn't felt that "in love" for years! I was in contact with him many times between May and June. Then my husband and I attended the "I Still Do" conference in June...and I know it was an appointment with God.

After coming home, I still struggled with the feelings for my old high school sweetheart. Still in contact with him by e-mail—which was my daily fix—I wasn't even feeling guilty for loving him still. Then, when I unwrapped that CD...and things changed. I heard you being interviewed on "Family Life Today"—hearing about your wife of sixteen years and six children (we have a Skye in our house too). Your testimony of God and your life story...and I realized that song, "I Still Do," would become the song that could change my heart toward my husband.

When I hear it, I realize how sacred and incredibly special the marriage covenant is. That song brought feelings that I had not felt in years back to the surface of my heart toward my husband. We have been married a little over six years. I have broken it off with my long-ago love. That song you wrote and sang will forever change my heart and marriage. I will listen to it every time I am tempted to run away from my husband and three little girls (ages 4, 3 and 1). Thank you for listening to God and being obedient to the call. Your testimony and song-writing ability have changed my life and saved my marriage. It's easy, when your parents divorce, to want to do the same...but hearing that you experienced the same made me realize how awesome it was for you to have made it 16 years with Julie. If you could do it, so could I!

A Country music artist who serves a mighty God! My husband and I have always planned to renew our vows at ten years...and we will play that song at our renewal ceremony. Why don't I just hire you to come and sing it!

—**Beth Ann K.**

❧ Knew Paul Back Then... ❧

You may or may not remember me. I can remember when you would come into Green Hills Executive Suites/Secretarial Services to use our typing service. I would type your lyrics for you, but you didn't have the money to pay for the services so you brought me some potato salad one day...To be honest, I didn't think that you would "make it." You were hanging out at one of the bars down off Division Street, drinking beer and tomato juice together. You proved me wrong. You are an inspiration to a lot of people, in more ways than one! Nice to listen to you on the radio. I hear your name a lot, and I always say to myself or someone, "I remember him, he stands out in my mind."

—**Anita B.; Nashville, Tennessee**

❧ The Perfect Instrument ❧

With great pride, I shared with my high school and GED students my knowledge of Paul Overstreet (the high school student). I then used "Billy Can't Read" and "Dig Another Well" as challenges to reach within themselves and seek the strength from God to become what God wants them to become. Paul's songs were the perfect instrument to let God's light shine in a public school classroom. Paul, you have made your old coach proud of you! God bless you.

—**Andy A.**
(Paul's former high school coach),
Newton, Mississippi

❧ A Light in the Darkness ❧

Growing up, it was my preference to listen to only Christian music. I never wanted to "defile" (jokingly, not legalistically) my stereo with anything else. I truly enjoyed and loved hearing and singing songs about the one Person who meant so much to me—Jesus Christ. Eventually I got married, only to find out that my husband did not share the same love for Christian music that I had. He enjoyed listening to music that I would find to be very depressing and degrading; songs that talked about lives that did not speak life to me. Eventually he began listening to Country music, and I found this to be a better selection, even though it wasn't what I considered the best selection. I still found the lyrics to be somewhat depressing and lifeless. Then I started hearing your music on the Country station, and I started asking, "Who is singing that song?" because the words were very sweet and not depressing. My husband informed me that it was you, and I have been a fan of yours ever since. Well, let's say that I am a fan of Jesus Christ, but you are by far my favorite Country music singer and songwriter, and I have praised God over and over for a light in the darkness. It was so refreshing to hear your music when I had no choice but to listen to the world's songs. Praise the Lord! God is so good.

—**Susan H.; Scottsdale, Pennsylvania**

✑ Life Lessons ✑

I am a great fan since the SKO days. Your songs and your life have been a wonderful witness and encouragement to me. In every interview I have seen you in, you have shown that God is first in your life, and that you love your wife and kids in a very special way.

When I was 26, I prayed and decided that I was not going to date any more, but wait on God for a man who would love God first and want a family as badly as I did. Listening to your songs helped me to believe that there was a man out there and that God would be faithful. I have to tell you it was a long wait, but your songs were a wonderful comfort and also kept my attitude in check. Your songs "There but for the Grace of God Go I" and "Dig Another Well" were very convincing. Your songs really taught me life lessons that I needed to learn. But one of my favorites is "Ball and Chain." That was my prayer, that God would give me a marriage and family like in that song. Well, after seven years, I met my husband. We were best friends for three years before he asked me to marry him. And, as God often does, He blessed me far more than I could have ever imagined. He is the most wonderful husband and the sweetest father to our two girls. They love him and are Daddy's girls. He even sings and plays the guitar. A special friend at my bridal shower made me a ball-and-chain cake; I had to explain to my husband's grandmother that it was not a joke but a very special gesture. Your songs are very special. Thank you for the hope and comfort that you and your music have been in my life.

Shannon A.

✑ Clean Country Music With Integrity ✑

I have been a long-time listener and lover of your music. When I was 25, I lost my husband, Jeff, to a work accident. He was 27 years old, and we had an almost 2-year old baby boy. Jeff loved all of your music. He was a Country boy, and while in his early twenties, he got saved, and then began to desire some clean Country music with integrity. After listening to your music, he was hooked. On our honeymoon, while in Pigeon Forge, Tennessee in February 1992, we danced in the parking lot of a Cracker Barrel restaurant to one of your songs. Your music really hit home to us.

We were involved in our small local church (as youth leaders and in evangelistic work). After Jeff's death in 1994, my life took some unexpected turns. There

were some really rough experiences and self-inflicted wounds. But I am a living tes-
timony that the love of your family and the love of the Lord can see you through
anything. My son, Jeffrey, is now seven years old. He looks and acts just like his
father. There is some real truth that the love and the blood of the father runs so
very deep. I pray my son will grow up to be a wonderful, godly man, like his father.

I am now remarried to a super guy. We live outside of Baton Rouge,
Louisiana, and we work very hard on our small farm. We have a hay-bailing and
bush-hogging business; he also works at the local paper mill. We have four chil-
dren between us, and so far, not any together yet. God has been so good to me.
He gave me a new start at life, and for that I am so very grateful. Your music
has meant so much to my family through all these years. Keep up the good work!

—Jennifer R-Y.

☞ Bosnia Report ☜

Thank you for coming over to Bosnia and giving one hell of a concert. It was
truly a great experience. Everyone here at Eagle Base who went to the show
just thought you were awesome. It is not every day that one gets to listen to good
Country music without all the unnecessary lights and smoke. I have always
enjoyed Randy Travis and his music, so I was pleasantly surprised to find out that
you had written my favorite songs by him. I have to say that I enjoyed the way
you sang them far more now than ever before. I had bought the two CDs that
were on sale at the concert, and they both kicked butt! We enjoyed your portion
of the show the most—the truth is: we never wanted you to leave the stage!

—Joe G.

☞ Music Transcends Religion, Race, Boundaries ☜

I am probably not your typical Paul Overstreet fan. I am a 46-year old Jew who
was born and raised in Brooklyn, New York. My father was a Holocaust survivor
who lost his entire family in World War II—seven brothers and sisters, as well as
both parents. When Auschwitz was liberated by the Allies, he weighed about 70
pounds, and spent several months recuperating in a Red Cross hospital.

He came to America in 1949, met my mom, and they raised a family. Since he was illiterate, he had to work very hard to provide us with the bare necessities. The first time I heard, "You Can't Stop Love" by RKO, I was totally blown away. That was pretty much the story of my dad's life (with some minor revisions). The way he felt about his family couldn't be changed by lack of money or opportunity. He was, to quote another of Paul's songs, "The Richest Man on Earth."

He passed away from lung cancer in 1992 at the age of 68, a few years after "Seein' My Father in Me" was written and performed by Paul on his "Sowin' Love" album. I listen to that song several times a week to this day, and think of my daddy, G-d bless his soul. After my mom died, he met and later married a Southern Baptist from Dalton, Georgia, while on a business trip. What an unlikely combination! But the marriage worked for both of them until his untimely demise.

He became an avid fan of Country music, especially Randy Travis. Need I say more? I would buy all of Randy's albums as gifts for him. I began to notice on the liner notes that all of the best songs were written by somebody named Paul Overstreet…who? Then I made the association with SKO, Tanya Tucker, Paul Davis, and the Judds, among others. I began to realize that this Overstreet fellow was a great songwriter, a teller of tales, a source of deep inspiration, a songwriter in the class of Lennon and McCartney, Richard Thompson, Sandy Denny, Ray Davies, Justin Hayward, and few others. He was in the elite—the pantheon. He had a special gift from G-d. He had the ability to make others feel what he felt, see what he saw, know what he knew.

The culmination of his artistic efforts was "Heroes," one of the greatest songs of the twentieth century. That was my dad. That was everyone's mama and daddy. We just never realized it before. Paul's music transcends religion, race and boundaries. It's summed up in his message to all of [us] that "Love Can Build a Bridge," regardless of whether we are black or white, Christian or Jew. Paul, keep on writing forever. The world needs you and your G-d-given gift.

—**Alan R.; Hartsdale, New York**

∾ Cowboy Poet ∾

*B*ack in Eucha, Oklahoma, a few years ago, my dad had cancer and was in the middle of a fight to maintain hope, develop deeper relationships with friends and family, take care of my mother who has a mental illness—he was much too *busy to deepen his relationship with his Maker. He was never one to appreciate mere sentiment, or to have too much stock in discussing feelings…or religion.*

His father was an orphan, a German immigrant who fell in hard times and left a son on the East Coast. My grandfather was shipped to the Midwest as farm help, and it was there he was given a new last name. Dad shared the same serious, hard-working nature and temper as Grandfather, but did not have the heart to continue the same hard discipline with his children.

Although I became a Christian while in high school, I never felt open to talk about "religion" with Dad, unless to answer some rare questions as when he wanted to make sure I was not getting "too strange." He did, however, enjoy a performance by my college church chorus, and one day asked me what my church thought of sin and conscience. I used that opportunity to share the gospel in a nutshell, and in return, was asked if I would help his mother—my grandmother— who, on her deathbed, needed encouragement. Dad felt I was a great help in putting her spirit at rest so she could leave us to see God with peace.

Although I listen to all kinds of music, I always gravitate to Country music, which has some of the best lyrics among any family-oriented or faith-oriented music. Whether it's about a tree in the back yard, never broken by the wind…the gift of love, love being deeper than the ocean…heroes…love that's not a ball and chain…or any other positive topic—this brand of "cowboy" music has been touching me for years, ever since I first heard it through the radio in my dad's garage as we worked on the old Ford. Even after receiving Master-level theology training, I find myself tuned to the Country station, listening to this brand of "praise music" encouraging me in secular, everyday life.

Unconsciously, my dad had a similar real connection to good Country music. I rarely buy a tape because only a few songs on any given album appeal to me. As far as I know, my dad has never purchased one, let alone one having religious overtone. When he did listen to music, it was most often upbeat Country. After discovering songs like "Heroes" on the radio, and seeing an interview with Paul Overstreet on a religious program, my appreciation for this songwriter's ministry brought even more joy to my heart. On a Father's Day—one of the few left for my dad—I gave him one gift: a cassette tape player with the song, "Seein' My Father in Me," cued first.

That song has brought me to tears on many occasions since I have dropped the youthful foolishness and resentment that a son can have towards his father. I learned to accept and love him, especially while his body grew tired and frail...yet his spirit, meanwhile, was growing, undaunted by his approaching death. His hands never ceased to help the community, family, and the volunteer fire department he helped to build. My appreciation for him grows now that he is gone. Every time I recognize his strength, character and mannerisms coming out in my own daily activities, I am touched again by my father's hand.

Dad was very quick to say how much he enjoyed the music, and asked me about the singer. I was anxious to tell him about the singer-writer who had such a wonderful view of life, and that he was a Christian. Dad, who had a disdain for religious things, said, "I don't know about that, but it sure is very good music." I was thrilled to provide him with the whole tape later, and it became not only the first popular album in his possession, but also the only one he would ever wear out in his truck. He let his friends listen to it when they rode together, and they talked a lot about it, especially, "If I Could Bottle This Up" and "Billy Can't Read"—a seeming contradiction to his tough nature. I can't help but believe he thought of Mother and he in their younger days as he listened to that song, and it helped him ease his mind on how difficult she had become.

This album became a pathway to talking with him on a deeper level, and a validation of him for the family values he cherished so much but could never talk about for fear of delving into religion. This music became his only cherished "praise album," although he would not call it such. On days when he could barely walk (due to chemo and radiation therapy), he drove himself to the hospital with the joy of life talked about in these tunes.

My wife, Sara, and I got word from Oklahoma that Dad was getting close to the end, and we again rushed by plane to see him in the Care Center where he waited for us. He was down from 160 pounds to 90, struggling to take every breath. He pulled himself up to an upright position and spoke: "I love you two"...his very last words on this tiny planet made only by God's love. We held his hand while he left, and were amazed by how much his hands resembled mine. I never stop seeing my father in me, and I also will have one album to encourage me through all of my future hard times.

Praise God for this singer/songwriter not controlled by the industry labels, this cowboy poet with a great preacher's voice and disciple's heart. He sings his message into the lives of the everyday person. Not so much in the church yard—more in the pasture, within earshot of lost sheep, goats, calves, bulls, and stallions.

—Dwight H.; Denver, Colorado

≈ They *Still Do* ≈

*J*ust wanted to say thanks for the song you wrote called, "I Still Do!" My wife, Stefani, and I were at the "I Still Do" conference at the Anaheim Pond in California. It was the first time we got to see you perform, and it was a treat. Stefani and I are playing your song as she walks down the aisle during our Renewal of Vows Ceremony. We got married at 18, and have been married ten years. We are dedicating our ceremony to Christ, and we tell everyone that Jesus is the reason we are still together. God bless you for all that you do.*

—Jason H.; California

≈ The "Secret" to Longevity ≈

*T*his story begins almost eight years ago, when our father was diagnosed with incurable cancer. He retired earlier than he would have liked so he could spend his remaining years doing what he enjoyed. The family wasn't sure what that was, but we soon found out. He started buying farm tractors at auctions and restoring them. After nearly eight years, he has kept the cancer at bay...and collected twenty some tractors in the process. This past year has been particularly rough because not only has his condition deteriorated, but our mom has developed some serious health problems too. She has always stood by him and tolerated many of his excesses because it was important that he be happy.*

This past Thanksgiving was their 45th wedding anniversary, and to be quite honest, this could be the last Thanksgiving we would all be together. So all ten of us kids got together and rented a banquet room at a local hotel so we could surprise them with an anniversary party, as well as having all their kids and sixteen grandkids together for Thanksgiving.

As you can probably guess, there were the expected prayers, thanks of appreciation, and "roasting" (paying ironic tributes). It was at this time, while one brother was roasting our dad, that he announced to the group he found the answer to what had puzzled us over the last couple of years. He said, "I've found the secret to Mom and Dad's longevity together: she thinks his tractors are sexy." At that, we all danced and sang to your song.

That's what happens when a song captures a moment. From now on, when any of us hear your song, we will be forever linked to a very special time in our family's life. You created a memory for us...and memories last forever. We hope that—by sharing this story with you—we can give something back to you. Thank you!

—Stuart V.; Bel Air, Maryland

More "Photos"

Paul and Julie attend a retreat with James and Shirley Dobson.

Paul and Julie with Jars of Clay in Australia.

Paul with Roy Rogers in Nashville.

Grand Ole Opry legend, Minnie Pearl, with Harmony and my niece Amy.

Paul, Julie and family with Mae Axton and Milton Berle.

Paul stands in front of his favorite car at a Nascar event in Bristol, Tennessee.

Paul with Franklin Graham.

Harry Warner, Julie Overstreet, Paul Overstreet, and Joyce Rice at the
45th Annual BMI Country Awards, September 23, 1997.

Epilogue

If you've read through this whole book, you realize that I am a Christian. And you realize that I believe God has made a big difference in my life, an important difference. My parents were Baptists—my father was a Baptist preacher—but they got divorced when I was very young. However, as I grew up, whether I was living with my mom or my dad, they always took me to church.

To be honest, I can't remember a time in my life when I didn't know who Jesus Christ was, or that I didn't know He was who He said He was. As a young boy I always wanted to go to church—I just had a desire to be near the things of God. As I grew older, I changed and developed a very cynical attitude. When I was a senior in high school, there was this minister who tried to reach out to me, but I just blew him off because I thought I knew more than he did. I'd been around churches long enough to think everyone in church was a hypocrite, and didn't want any part of it.

The thing about God is: He'll let you go along with your cynical thinking as long as you want. You can use other people's shortcomings for your excuse not to do what He has designed for you to do, and He'll let you do it. But He *will* catch up with you sometime!

When I started in the music business, I was smoking marijuana, drinking alcohol, doing cocaine when I could afford it. I had grown accustomed to substance abuse by hanging out with people who did it. They were stars…the music industry had become my god…and I thought, "Well, hey, if the music industry said it's okay, then I can do it and be successful."

Of course, this was contrary to what *I said* I believed as a Christian. At the studios, they'd light up a joint and pass it around, but when it would get to me, I would say, "No, I don't want it." Then they'd say, "What's wrong with you, when did you turn into being a born-again Christian?" So I would take the joint…and then I would be so angry with myself for my weakness.

The cocaine thing really had an impact on me. When people do cocaine, they line it up on a mirror. I used to look at my face in that mirror, and I'd think, "Man, what has happened to you? You used to be the guy who loves life. You used to be an athlete, playing football, critical of people who did drugs while they were playing." That was the guy I used to be—now I had become the guy snorting cocaine.

It came to a point where I hated music, I hated myself, I hated everything I was doing. I was very confused. By the time I was about 28, I had hit bottom—with the drugs, and the alcohol, and all—and with trying to figure out how to have success in the music industry. It was kind of a strange place to be, because I had done everything there was to do, but nothing brought me happiness. I'd had some success with some of my songs, I had new cars and all sorts of things. I was into drugs and alcohol, I had been married briefly and divorced, I had lots of girlfriends…but I just came to the point where I wasn't happy.

So I decided to release the control of my life to Christ. I prayed, "Lord, I've made such a mess out of my life, I don't know what to do. I don't see anything else out there to do, I just think it looks like it's kind of over." I was ready to give it all up. I basically took the whole music, song-writing, performing, the guitar, everything…and just "laid it on the altar" to God and said, "It's all Yours."

I didn't kick the marijuana habit all at once, but there was a turning point one day when—with the help of God—I *did* just stop using it. It was a decision I made…but I also knew that God had set me free. He gave me the strength to say "no" to something I had been fighting for a long time. Drugs were a dead-end road, of no value in my life.

As for cocaine, that was a little different. I was hanging out with an old friend in a room at a studio, and he gave me some of his cocaine "to help us write better." You never know what sort of stuff people would have—

some of it can be pretty dangerous, lots of people have died from it. I snorted it, and we were sitting there trying to write...and I started having this really horrible feeling. My chest got tight, breathing was a little difficult, and I felt very weird. I got up, walked outside, and standing in the parking lot, I started praying.

I said, "Lord, I'm not ready. If for some reason my life were to end right now, I'm not ready to go." Most everything I'd done in my life up to that point had felt it was all for selfish reasons. I expressed that to God, saying, "Lord, I really want to change things, I want to do things differently." And I felt a peace come over me. My body relaxed, my chest calmed down. I didn't even go back inside to say goodbye or anything, I just got into my car and went home. From that point on, I never touched the stuff again. I was suddenly sober, my mind was straight, my body was at peace, and I knew that God had intervened right then! I made a conscious decision to walk away from my old life and walk toward God.

This is something for everyone—I am no different from you. Don't say, "Well, look at what God did for him. He's a writer, he's important. God isn't going to do that for me." That's not what the Word of God says! It says that every single person is created by God for a reason, and He wants to show Himself to them so they too can find that reason. God's Word is filled with His love and His wisdom for His children. The whole Book of Proverbs is written like a father talking to his child—or the king talking to the prince. It starts off:

> *My son, hear the instruction of your father...to know wisdom and instruction, to perceive the words of understanding, to receive the instruction of wisdom, justice, judgment, and equity...A wise man will hear and increase learning, and a man of understanding will attain wise counsel...The fear of the Lord is the beginning of knowledge, but fools despise wisdom and instruction (Proverbs 1:8,2-7).*

If I'm going to consider myself the child of God—someone who is important to Him—shouldn't I read His Word as though it's talking to me? I said, "If I'm going to be drunk all the time, then I'm going to be in poverty, because the Word says, 'Hear, my son, and be wise; and guide your heart in the way. Do not mix with winebibbers, or with gluttonous eaters of meat; for the drunkard and the glutton will come to poverty'" (Prov. 23:19-21a). That was a warning for me—and it is a warning for you. God will do for *anyone* what He did for me. It is His desire that you are sober, that you are in the right frame of mind. He *will* deliver anyone who asks Him.

I try to write songs about real-life things, that will encourage people, motivate them to be positive. Some people say these songs are hokey...but there is a really thin line between being maudlin and one-dimensional—and actually saying something upbeat, with real meaning. I wouldn't talk about my drug problems if they were still part of me...but now I enjoy being able to say, "Hey, I've been there and I understand what it feels like...but there is hope, there *is* a cure—and it is found in Jesus Christ!"

A lot of my songs come out of my own life. When I wrote *"Same Ole Me,"* I was still involved in drugs, and alcohol, and stuff like that. But God is the One who gave me the idea for this song...and He was giving me a pattern for my life. It was sort of "prophetic"—that God was going to give me a woman who I would love all of my life, even when we both get old and gray:

> *"My face is wrinkled but my blue eyes still sparkle*
> *With the love I felt for you the day we met.*
> *To me, you're just as lovely as the first time I saw you.*
> *I'm still the same ole me, loving the same sweet you.*
> *Time hasn't withered our hearts.*
> *And when our days are through, I'll still be loving you;*
> *Even death can't keep us apart."*

I sort of argued with God about the "wholesome" songs I was writing, but He gave me His assurance, and so I said, "Well, okay, I'll keep doing whatever You say." The next thing I knew, my songs were all over the radio...and God was right on target! It wasn't my brilliance—I was just trying to be obedient. God allowed me to see the fruit of being sober, of having—as the Bible says—"a sound mind" (3 Jn. 2).

This book is my story about my songs. God gave them to me to help me work through some issues in my own life, to see where He wanted me to go with my wife and our family. But way more than that—He has used them to bless other people's lives, to speak into their hearts His own words of love and hope, and forgiveness and restoration of lost dreams. This makes me different from a lot of other Country music writers, but that's okay—the world needs people who see things differently. I am a Christian *and* I am a Country music writer—that's who God made me to be. And I'm glad.

> *If I speak with human eloquence and angelic ecstasy but don't love, I'm nothing but the creaking of a rusty gate. If I speak God's Word with power, revealing all His mysteries and making everything plain as day, and if I have faith that says to a mountain, "Jump," and it jumps, but I don't love, I'm nothing. If I give everything I own to the poor and even go to the stake to be burned as a martyr, but I don't love, I've gotten nowhere. So, no matter what I say, what I believe, and what I do, I'm bankrupt without love* (I Corinthians 13:1-3, *The Message* [Copyright © 1993, 1994, 1995 by Eugene H. Peterson. Published by NavPress]).

> *For God did not send His Son into the world to condemn the world, but that the world through Him might be saved...For God so loved the world that He gave His only begotten Son, that whoever believes in Him should not perish but have everlasting life* (John 3:17,16).

Complete Listing of Paul Overstreet Songs

"A Long Line of Love"…1986…with Thom Schuyler…recorded by Michael
Martin Murphy…Top Ten song

"All the Fun"…1988…with Taylor Dunn…recorded by Paul Overstreet….
Top Ten song

"Ball and Chain"…1990…with Don Schlitz…recorded by Paul Overstreet

"Be Mine"…1999…with Paul Davis…recorded by Paul Overstreet

"Billy Can't Read"…1990…with Jerry Michael…recorded by
Paul Overstreet

"Blackberry Cobbler"…1995…recorded by Paul Overstreet

"Call the Preacher"…1988…recorded by Paul Overstreet

"(The) Calm at the Center of My Storm"…1990…with Don Schlitz…
recorded by Paul Overstreet

"Daddy's Come Around (to Mama's Way of Thinking)"…1990…with
Don Schlitz…recorded by Paul Overstreet

"Deeper Than the Holler"…1986…with Don Schlitz…recorded by
Randy Travis

"Dig Another Well"…1988…with Al Gore and Nat Stucky…recorded by
Randy Travis…Top Ten song

"Even When It Don't Feel Like It"…1995…recorded by Paul Overstreet

"Everybody Needs Your Touch"…1999…with Rob Crosby…recorded by Paul Overstreet

"Everywhere We Go"…with Bill Aerts…recorded by Kenny Chesney…Top Ten song

"Forever and Ever, Amen"…1986…with Don Schlitz…recorded by Randy Travis…1987 *Academy of Country Music* Song of the Year/ 1988 *National Association of Recording Arts & Sciences* Grammy/ 1988 *Country Music Association* Song of the Year/ 1988 The Nashville Network Viewers Choice Award

"God Is Good (All the Time)"…1999…with Don Moen…recorded by Paul Overstreet and Don Moen

"He Is Risen"…1986…recorded by Paul Overstreet

"Head Over Heels"…1992…with Paul Davis… recorded by Paul Overstreet

"Heart of My Heart"…1986…recorded by Paul Overstreet

"Heaven Is a Place I'm Gonna Go"…1986…recorded by Paul Overstreet

"Heroes"…1990…with Claire Cloninger…recorded by Paul Overstreet

"(She Wants to Be a) Homemaker"…1988…with Dan Tyler…recorded by Paul Overstreet

"I Always Will"…1995…with Archie Jordan…recorded by Paul Overstreet

"I Fell in Love Again Last Night"…1982…with Thom Schuyler…recorded by the Forester Sisters

"I Still Do"…1999…with Billy Aerts…recorded by Paul Overstreet

"I Will Carry My Cross for You"…1986…recorded by Paul Overstreet

"I Won't Take Less Than Your Love"…1986…with Don Schlitz…recorded by Tanya Tucker, Paul Overstreet, and Paul Davis…Top Ten song

"If I Could Bottle This UP"…1990…with Dean Dillon…recorded by Paul Overstreet

"I'm Gonna Ring Her"…1995…with Randy Travis…recorded by Paul Overstreet

"I'm So Glad I Was Dreaming"…1990…with Don Schlitz…recorded by Paul Overstreet

"Just Like Jesus"…1986…recorded by Paul Overstreet

"Let's Go to Bed Early"…1995…with Taylor Dunn and Sean McCarthy… recorded by Paul Overstreet

"Living by The Book"…1999…with Doug Stone…recorded by Paul Overstreet

"Lord, She Sure Is Good at Loving Me"…1992…with Randy Travis… recorded by Paul Overstreet

"Lost and Found"…1986…recorded by Paul Overstreet

"Love Helps Those Who Cannot Help Themselves"…1988…recorded by SKO…Top Ten song

"Love Can Build a Bridge"…1990…with Naomi Judd and John Jarvis…recorded by the Judds…1992 Grammy (for songwriter), Top Ten song

"Love Is Strong"…1992…with Archie Jordan…recorded by Paul Overstreet…1992 Dove Award Country Recorded Album of the Year

"Love Lives On"…1990…with Taylor Dunn…recorded by Paul Overstreet

"Love Never Sleeps"…1987…recorded by Paul Overstreet

"Merry Christmas, Mary"…1987…with Don Schlitz…recorded by Paul Overstreet

"Mr. Miller"…1995…recorded by Paul Overstreet

"Me and My Baby"…1992…with Paul Davis…recorded by Paul Overstreet

"My Arms Stay Open All Night"…1989…with Don Shclitz…recorded by Tanya Tucker…Top ten song

"My Rock"…1983…with Claude Hensley and Don F. Bryant…recorded by Paul Overstreet

"'Neath the Light of Your Love"…1988…with Don Shclitz…recorded by Paul Overstreet

"Oh Why"…1986…with Thom Schuyler…recorded by Paul Overstreet

"On the Other Hand"…1986…with Don Schlitz…recorded by
   Randy Travis…1986 *Academy of Country Music* Song of the Year/ 1987
   Music City News Traditional Song of the Year/ 1987 *Country Music
   Association* Song of the Year

"One in a Million"…1995…with Tom Cambell…recorded by
   Paul Overstreet…*Academy of Country Music* Song of the Year

"One Love At a Time"…1985…with Paul Davis…recorded by
   Tanya Tucker…Top Ten song

"Richest Man on Earth"…1988…with Don Schlitz…recorded by
   Paul Overstreet…Top Five song

"Same Ole Me"…1981…recoreded by Randy Travis, George Jones…
   Top Five song

"Seein' My Father in Me"…1988…with Taylor Dunn…recorded by
   Paul Overstreet…1991 *Gospel Music Association* Dove Award for
   Country Recorded Song of the Year/ # One Country Song

"She Supports Her Man"…1989…recorded by Paul Overstreet

"She Thinks My Tractor's Sexy"…1999…with Jim Collins…recorded by
   Kenny Chesney

"Sowin' Love"…1988…with Don Schlitz…recorded by Paul Overstreet….
   Top Ten song

"Steady Working"…1999…recorded by Paul Overstreet

"Still Out There Swinging"…1992…recorded by Paul Overstreet

"Straight and Narrow"…1988…with Don Schlitz…recorded by
   Paul Overstreet

"Take Another Run"…1992…with Don Schlitz…recorded by
   Paul Overstreet

"Take Some Action"….1992…with Tom Campbell…recorded by
   Paul Overstreet

"The Day My Daddy Didn't Come Home"…2000…with Alan Shamblin

"There But for the Grace of God Go I"…1992…with Taylor Dunn…
   recorded by Paul Overstreet…Dove Award Country Recorded
   Song of the Year

"'Til the Mountains Disappear"...1990...with Don Schlitz...recorded by
Paul Overstreet

"Toughest Battles"...1999...with Eddie Reddick...recorded by
Paul Overstreet

"Until We Know"...1986...recorded by Paul Overstreet

"We've Got to Keep On Meeting Like This"...1995...with Archie Jordan...
recorded by Paul Overstreet

"What Are Friends For"...1998...with Alan Shamblin...recorded by
Paul Overstreet

"What God Has Joined Together"...1988...with Paul Davis...recorded by
Paul Overstreet

"What's Going Without Saying"...1992...with Jeff Borders...recorded by
Paul Overstreet

"When Mama Ain't Happy"...1999...recorded by Paul Overstreet

"When You Say Nothing at All"...1988...with Don Schlitz...recorded by
Keith Whitley, Alison Krause, Ronan Keating...Top Ten song

"Wise Men Still Seek Him"...1999...with Taylor Dunn...recorded by
Paul Overstreet

"You Gave Me Time"...1996...with Bob Shapiro...recorded by
Paul Overstreet

Resources

Discography

1986—**Lost and Found:** *Heart of My Heart...Lost and Found...Heaven Is a Place I'm Gonna Go...Until We Know...Oh Why...Just Like Jesus...I Will Carry My Cross for You...He Is Risen* (Necessity Records)

1989—**Sowin' Love:** *Love Helps Those...All the Fun...Call the Preacher...Richest Man on Earth...Sowin' Love...Love Never Sleeps...Dig Another Well...Seein' My Father in Me...What God Has Joined Together...Homemaker...'Neath the Light of Your Love* (BMG Music; RCA Corporation)

1990—**Heroes:** *Ball and Chain...If I Could Bottle This Up...Daddy's Come Around...Love Lives On...Heroes...I'm So Glad I Was Dreaming...Straight and Narrow...Billy Can't Read...She Supports Her Man...'Til the Mountains Disappear...The Calm at the Center of My Storm* (BMG Music; RCA Corporation)

1992—**Love Is Strong:** *Take Another Run...Still Out There Swinging...Me and My Baby...There But for the Grace of God Go I...Love Is Strong...Head Over Heels...What's Going Without Saying...Take Some Action...Lord, She Sure Is Good at Loving Me...'Til the Answer Comes* (BMG Music; RCA Corporation)

1994—**The Best of Paul Overstreet:** *Sowin' Love...All the Fun...Seein' My Father in Me...Richest Man on Earth...Daddy's Come Around...Heroes...Ball and Chain...If I Could Bottle This Up...Billy Can't Read...Take Another Run* (The RCA Record Label)

1996—*Time:* *We've Got to Keep On Meeting Like This...I'm Gonna Ring Her...Even When It Don't Feel Like It...Let's Go to Bed Early...You Gave Me Time...I Always Will...One in a Million...Blackberry Cobbler...Mr. Miller...My Rock* (Scarlet Moon Records)

1999—*A Songwriter's Project—Volume One:* *Same Ole Me...I Won't Take Less Than Your Love...When You Say Nothing at All...Forever and Ever, Amen...A Long Line of Love...Diggin' Up Bones...Be Mine...On the Other Hand...I Fell in Love Again Last Night...Toughest Battles...What Are Friends For?...When Mama Ain't Happy* (Scarlet Moon Records)

2000—*Living by The Book:* *Lost and Found...He Is Risen...Dig Another Well...Everybody Needs Your Touch...Living by The Book...Steady Working...Oh Why...I Will Carry My Cross for You...God Is Good...Until We Know...Heart of My Heart...Wise Men Still Seek Him...I Won't Take Less Than Your Love* (Scarlet Moon Records)

Videology

All the Fun (RCA)

Seein' My Father in Me (RCA)

Heroes (RCA)

Billy Can't Read (RCA)

Take Another Run at It, Baby (RCA)

Even When It Don't Feel Like It (Integrity Records)

When Mama Ain't Happy (Scarlet Moon Records)

Forever and Ever, Amen (Warner Brothers)

A Long Line of Love (Warner Brothers)

When You Say Nothing at All (Rounder Records/RCA)

Paul's Picks

I work with a lot of excellent organizations and ministries that are making a difference in our world, and I am glad to be able to recommend them to you!

Samaritan's Purse

One of the joys of my life has been working with my friend, Franklin Graham, the president of Samaritan's Purse. This ministry is an international relief organization committed to meeting the spiritual and physical needs of people in crisis situations. I have traveled with Samaritan's Purse to different countries around the world. This organization rapidly responds to places like Nicaragua, Honduras, and Kosovo by providing services such as food, shelter, clothing, and healthcare in their time of need. What really excites me is that their work is motivated by a compelling desire to share the good news of God's gospel, which is exhibited by Franklin's crusades, as well as the incredible ministry of Samaritan's Purse.

For more information about Samaritan's Purse, go online to:

www.samaritan.org/

Write: **Samaritan's Purse**, P.O. Box 3000, Boone, North Carolina, 28607, USA; or call: 828-262-1980.

Literacy Volunteers of America

For more information about Literacy Volunteers of America, go online to:

www.literacyvolunteers.org/home/

Write: **Literacy Volunteers of America, Inc.**, 635 James Street, Syracuse, New York, 13203-2214; or call: 315-474-0001 or 1-800-223-8813.

Family Life

Founded in 1976, Family Life is a non-profit organization devoted to effectively developing godly families one home at a time. More than two million radio listeners tune in to *Family Life Today* radio broadcasts. In the year 2000, 80, 863 people attended regional marriage and parenting conferences, and 58,000 attended the "I Still Do" conferences. Dennis Rainey has been the executive director for 25 years.

Kids Across America

Kids Across America seeks to provide a life changing camping experience for urban teenagers through three Kids Across America Kamps (KAA) on the shores of Table Rock Lake in Southwest Missouri. These camps are decidedly Christian in focus and philosophy and combine sporting activities with Christian teaching to help develop character qualities and leadership skills in the hearts and minds of urban teens. KAA also emphasizes the tremendous importance of working with the adult urban leaders who come to camp from all over the country as mentors for the youth. In fact, part of the KAA staff is dedicated to encouraging, training and teaching these adult urban leaders.

In 1978, Joe White of Kanakuk Kamps, Inc., the largest family of Christian sports camps in America, started giving the last week of camp in the summer to serve the camping needs of inner-city youth. Kids Across America Foundation, a 501(c)(3) non-profit organization was birthed out of this need, and eventually the demand for a camp dedicated to serving urban youth and inner city leaders became so great that the first Kids Across America camp was built. It was completed in 1991, and in 1995 KAA 2 was completed adjacent to KAA 1. The number of young people and inner city leaders served has grown every year, and this demand has led to plans to open another camp, KAA 3, in the summer of 2001. In September of 2000, the IGÇÖm Third Foundation was renamed Kids Across America.

During the summer of 2001, KAA will host nearly 6,000 urban teenagers and approximately 800 inner city adult leaders at three camp facilities. They will come from over 25 states and 90 cities, including Chicago, St. Louis, Detroit, Memphis, Little Rock, Dallas and Houston. Additionally, a Leadership Training Camp, Higher Ground, opened in 1998 and will annually train 180 young urban leaders in the biblical servant leadership principles necessary to impact their communities for Jesus Christ.

Campers are given the opportunity to enjoy 30 different sports and activities, meet new friends, build relationships with a staff of 500 caring counselors (many of whom are college athletes), and be exposed to the message of hope in Jesus Christ. Their camp experience often provides the catalyst for a changed life and the beginning of a mentoring relationship with a dedicated adult.

Sessions run for 8 or 9 days at KAA 1, KAA 2, and KAA 3, and for 8, 9, and 16 days at Higher Ground. The tuition charge for each camper is about 20 percent of the actual cost. The various youth organizations usually have fund raising activities to help their campers meet tuition charges.

Kids Across America raises the other 80 percent through the generous support of donors throughout the country. KAA is overseen by an independent seven member Board of Directors and is a member of the Evangelical Council for Financial Accountability (ECFA), Christian Camping International (CCI), and the Christian Community Development Association (CCDA). As the numbers of young people and leaders served through the camps has grown, KAA has also grown in the scope of support services provided throughout the year. One service provided is a leadership development program called *Champions* and *Women of Destiny*. As a result of the annual need for scholarship assistance and the continued growth of the services provided, additional sources of financial support for this ministry are always welcome.

For More Information

Write to:

Scarlet Moon Records
P.O. Box 320
Pegram, TN 37143

e-mail:

pauloverstreet@pauloverstreet.com

Phone and Fax:

Phone: 1+615-952-3999
FAX: 1+615-952-3151

Music by Paul Overstreet

A Songwriter's Project / Volume 1

Paul has just released what he calls *A Songwriter's Project* as a songwriter, artist and producer. This has been a labor of love, and much awaited by those who will love Overstreet's own rendering of his hit songs previously recorded by other artists. "When You Say Nothing at All"…"Forever and Ever, Amen"…"On the Other Hand"…"I Fell in Love Again Last Night" plus eight more.

Living by The Book

Living by The Book is Paul's newest offering of Christian songs. Here's what Franklin Graham says about this album: "His Christian songs are some of the best ever written. I'm excited about this new album. It's great. I Love It." Titles like "Lost and Found"…"Dig Another Well"…"Until We Know"…"God Is Good"…"Oh Why" and eight more.

The Best of Paul Overstreet

A great compilation of some of Paul's greatest songs, like "Sowin' Love"…"Seein' My Father in Me"…"Heroes"…and the nationally-acclaimed piece on literacy, "Billy Can't Read." Undeniably *The Best of Paul Overstreet*.

To purchase other product by Paul Overstreet visit your local bookstore or purchase from Paul's web site at:

www.pauloverstreet.com

Additional copies of this book and other
book titles from DESTINY IMAGE are
available at your local bookstore.

For a complete list of our titles,
visit us at www.destinyimage.com
Send a request for a catalog to:

Destiny Image® Publishers, Inc.

P.O. Box 310
Shippensburg, PA 17257-0310

*"Speaking to the Purposes of God for This
Generation and for the Generations to Come"*

Exciting titles
by Don Nori

➤ NO MORE SOUR GRAPES

Who among us wants our children to be free from the struggles we have had to bear? Who among us wants the lives of our children to be full of victory and love for their Lord? Who among us wants the hard-earned lessons from our lives given freely to our children? All these are not only possible, they are also God's will. You can be one of those who share the excitement and joy of seeing your children step into the destiny God has for them. If you answered "yes" to these questions, the pages of this book are full of hope and help for you and others just like you.
ISBN 0-7684-2037-7

➤ THE POWER OF BROKENNESS

Accepting Brokenness is a must for becoming a true vessel of the Lord, and is a stepping-stone to revival in our hearts, our homes, and our churches. Brokenness alone brings us to the wonderful revelation of how deep and great our Lord's mercy really is. Join this companion who leads us through the darkest of nights. Discover the *Power of Brokenness*.
ISBN 1-56043-178-4

➤ THE ANGEL AND THE JUDGMENT

Few understand the power of our judgments—or the aftermath of the words we speak in thoughtless, emotional pain. In this powerful story about a preacher and an angel, you'll see how the heavens respond and how the earth is changed by the words we utter in secret.
ISBN 1-56043-154-7

➤ HIS MANIFEST PRESENCE

This is a passionate look at God's desire for a people with whom He can have intimate fellowship. Not simply a book on worship, it faces our triumphs as well as our sorrows in relation to God's plan for a dwelling place that is splendid in holiness and love.
ISBN 0-914903-48-9
Also available in Spanish.
ISBN 1-56043-079-6

➤ SECRETS OF THE MOST HOLY PLACE

Here is a prophetic parable you will read again and again. The winds of God are blowing, drawing you to His Life within the Veil of the Most Holy Place. There you begin to see as you experience a depth of relationship your heart has yearned for. This book is a living, dynamic experience with God!
ISBN 1-56043-076-1

➤ HOW TO FIND GOD'S LOVE

Here is a heartwarming story about three people who tell their stories of tragedy, fear, and disease, and how God showed them His love in a real way.
ISBN 0-914903-28-4
Also available in Spanish.
ISBN 1-56043-024-9

Available at your local Christian bookstore.

For more information and sample chapters, visit www.reapernet.com

Books to help you grow strong in Jesus

➤ **SECRET SOURCES OF POWER**

by T.F. Tenney with Tommy Tenney.

Everyone is searching for power. People are longing for some external force to empower their lives and transform their circumstances. *Secret Sources of Power* furnishes some of the keys that will unlock the door to Divine power. You might be surprised at what is on the other side of that door. It will be the opposite of the world's concepts of power and how to obtain it. You will discover that before you lay hold of God's power you must let go of your own resources. You will be challenged to go down before you can be lifted up. Death always comes before resurrection. If you are dissatisfied with your life and long for the power of God to be manifested in you then now is the time. Take the keys and open the door to *Secret Sources of Power!*

ISBN 0-7684-5000-4

➤ **THE GOD CHASERS** (National Best-Seller)

by Tommy Tenney.

There are those so hungry, so desperate for His presence, that they become consumed with finding Him. Their longing for Him moves them to do what they would otherwise never do: Chase God. But what does it really mean to chase God? Can He be "caught"? Is there an end to the thirsting of man's soul for Him? Meet Tommy Tenney—God chaser. Join him in his search for God. Follow him as he ignores the maze of religious tradition and finds himself, not chasing God, but to his utter amazement, caught by the One he had chased.

ISBN 0-7684-2016-4

Also available in Spanish

ISBN 0-7899-0642-2

➤ **GOD CHASERS DAILY MEDITATION & PERSONAL JOURNAL**

by Tommy Tenney.

ISBN 0-7684-2040-7

➤ **GOD'S FAVORITE HOUSE**

by Tommy Tenney.

The burning desire of your heart can be fulfilled. God is looking for people just like you. He is a Lover in search of a people who will love Him in return. He is far more interested in you than He is interested in a building. He would hush all of Heaven's hosts to listen to your voice raised in heartfelt love songs to Him. This book will show you how to build a house of worship within, fulfilling your heart's desire and His!

ISBN 0-7684-2043-1

➤ **THE LOST PASSIONS OF JESUS**

by Donald L. Milam, Jr.

What motivated Jesus to pursue the cross? What inner strength kept His feet on the path laid before Him? Time and tradition have muted the Church's knowledge of the passions that burned in Jesus' heart, but if we want to—if we dare to—we can still seek those same passions. Learn from a close look at Jesus' own life and words and from the writings of other dedicated followers the passions that enflamed the Son of God and changed the world forever!

ISBN 0-9677402-0-7

Available at your local Christian bookstore.